Christian Spiritual Ecology

Christian Spiritual Ecology

A New Approach to the Human/Nature Relationship

MITCHELL NELSON

WIPF & STOCK · Eugene, Oregon

CHRISTIAN SPIRITUAL ECOLOGY
A New Approach to the Human/Nature Relationship

Wipf & Stock
An Imprint of Wipf and Stock Publishers
199 W. 8th Ave., Suite 3
Eugene, OR 97401

www.wipfandstock.com

PAPERBACK ISBN: 979-8-3852-5702-7
HARDCOVER ISBN: 979-8-3852-5703-4
EBOOK ISBN: 979-8-3852-5704-1

He was with God in the beginning, Through him all things were made; without him nothing was made that has been made.

—JOHN 1:2–3

Contents

Introduction

As you read this book, I hope there is a sense of peace with you. That peace you feel when you get to the coastline and look out onto the water, the peace you feel when you walk into the woods and smell the scents of the trees and earth, or the peace you feel entering a garden and hearing the sounds of the pollinators and birds singing. This peace in my own belief is the presence of Jesus and his resurrection along with the presence of God right there present in something we are experiencing.

Throughout my education in the combined love for Jesus and natural world I looked for works that directly spoke to that presence of God and Jesus in the natural world in an encouragement of that as a spiritual practice and found more theoretical work that had a need to fit in with past Christian theologies. This led to my creating of this work.

There is no claim here that this is solely a Christian experience. Having an ecological relationship with God and nature, I am sure many types of religions and the nonreligious can also speak about their own spiritual ecology. The reason for writing this work in particular for Christians is because in theology we have really struggled with speaking directly to that experience of God and Jesus in a relationship with nature.

The obvious need that is the focus of this book is the research into the current deficiency in our human/nature relationship and the negative effects this is having on humanity as part of the natural world and on the natural world itself. The new creative response is for Christians to feel confident about worshiping God in nature through a relationship with Jesus. In order to make this model work, this work focuses on the study of ecology, which is the study of relationships between living organisms. In effect we will be looking at the human/nature relationship that is suffering from separation. In particular, we will explore scientific research on the benefits of time spent developing the human/nature relationship for humanity and the natural world.

We will start with a discussion on why we have not allowed our Christian thinking to progress with historical and scientific research of our time in the same way most fields of thought progress with the current research. From there we will give the foundation in the definition of the ecological relationship.

With that foundation in place, we then move to look at the spiritual writings of Thurman, Muir, and Celtic Christianity that help us envision what this ecology looks like for Christians. These individuals directly spoke to a spiritual enrichment with God and Jesus in nature. Their own impact through their spirituality on humanity and nature helps us to realize how vital and important this spiritual ecology is for Christians.

Next, we build on this ecology by supporting it with the scientific research on the cognitive and physical health benefits of practicing this ecology by spending time in nature. What was described as self-realization from these practitioners is then supported with actual scientific data that there is a benefit for humanity to practice this ecology. The self-realization here in scientific terms is described as biophilia, which states that humans have a biological need to interact with the natural world.

With this ecology in place with definition and understanding of the relational practice we turn to look at why this is becoming less of a practice in our society in general, with research on the indoor generation that will now spend 90 percent of their lives indoors not practicing this ecology. From there we will discuss the ecology as togetherness rather than the separation narrative and move it forward into concepts of healing humanity and the natural world through the practice of this CSE.

As this work is continued forward, we propose the future of CSE within our churches as a model of ministry. I then conclude with particular points of what this spiritual practice has to offer in alignment with Jesus' teachings and the Gospels. In conclusion, these points of the practice will enable the reader to begin to contemplate their individual CSE that aligns with their own individual setting.

Peace to you and your reading,
Mitch

Chapter 1: What Is Christian Spiritual Ecology?

THE PROBLEMATIC OF CHRISTIAN THOUGHT NOT PROGRESSING WITH THE CURRENT RESEARCH

Those of us in the United States or the broader Western contemporary world live in a culture that bases much of its knowledge in the sciences. Nevertheless, our Christian theologies often fail to relate coherently to the progression of the sciences. When our theology is based in the science of a thousand years ago, it simply does not align with the current state of scientific knowledge. It is a positive that scientific knowledge changes progressively over time, as noted by Amy Crawford in an article entitled "Good Science Changes: That's a Good Thing." She writes: "Throughout history, the process of discovery has involved correcting mistakes."[1] However, with regard to the human/nature relationship, our Christian theology has not progressed along with the scientific research and corrected ancient mistakes.

Most fields of study follow a natural progression of change in their understanding, and they do so for the betterment of that field. There then follows a betterment for the aspect of society affected by that field of study. Thus, in filmmaking, where we have seen progress in camera equipment from Edison's kinetoscope to sophisticated digital filming devises, it would be ridiculous to

1. Crawford, "Good Science Changes."

suggest that because the original filmmakers used the kinetoscope, contemporary filmmakers should use one as well. Similarly, it would be ridiculous to require a certain scientific field to use only the tools and instruments from two hundred years ago.

For various reasons, acceptance of scientific progress has not occurred when it comes to Christian theology. We tend to stack one doctrine on top of the other instead of letting the current research affect what was believed in the past. A good example of this is the biblical canon, and the early belief, when it was first established, that the author of the Gospel of John and the author of the book of Revelation were the same person. This was why Revelation was included in the first place. The early church historian Eusebius disagreed.[2] He was the first to note that differences in style and underlying theology indicated that the two authors were in fact different. But because the canon was already established, the book of Revelation remained, even though the sort of God the book presents is very different from the loving and living God of the Gospel of John. And the sort of Jesus presented is very different also.

In our time, thinking among scholars distinguishing the different biblical authors based on content, theological views, writing style, and for other technical reasons has become increasingly commonplace.[3] Nevertheless, very few suggest altering the canon. This reluctance stems from the way we cling to our traditions and doctrines, even if those traditions have harmful implications, or if they are inherently contradictory. This sort of unwillingness to change along with changes in knowledge has contributed to problems in the understanding of the relationship between humanity and nature that I address and seek to correct in this book.

We still read the Bible and try to design Christian ecologies as if the Gospel of John, which teaches about a loving God and a complete resurrection of Jesus, were not a completely different ending from that of the book of Revelation, where God is someone to fear and Jesus is removed from creation. These two different

2. Just, "On the Authorship."

3. Marina, "Who Wrote the Book of Revelation?"

endings affect how a Christian understands ecology, and if the New Testament had ended after John's Gospel, there is implied a different ecology in that ending.

Because Christianity is a religion based upon traditions, and because many of our traditions are considered sacred, we tend to pull back from changing any aspect of them. Yet does questioning an underlying theory detract from the sacredness of our tradition? Another such underlying theology is the concept of original sin derived from Augustine. This doctrine is very problematic when applied to ecology, and yet has remained relatively unchecked by Christians for centuries.

From the perspective of ecology, this doctrine actually diminishes the sacredness of God's creation, and we find Christians trying to fit outdated notions like this one into their ecotheologies and ecologies. In response, this work is an attempt to move us past those outdated theologies so that, along with the sciences, Christians can begin to have healthy ecological dialogues about the nature/humanity relationship, and to do so in a way that can be aligned with the Gospels and with the teachings of Jesus.

A cosmology is a theory or doctrine that describes the natural order of the universe. Augustine's doctrine of original sin gives us a cosmology in which the universe and creation are corrupt and human beings have a sinful nature. In Hebrew, the word "sin" means to miss the mark of God or to be separated from God. So, this cosmology from Augustine places the natural world and humanity in a godless state in their very essence. Interestingly, ending the Bible with the book of Revelation gives us a very similar cosmology, in that in this text God has become a God to fear rather than the loving God Jesus teaches us about. Also in this text, Jesus is removed from the earth instead of being resurrected and present within creation as the Author of Life. Here again we find a cosmology that places the human/nature relationship in a godless state of chaos.

In contrast, the cosmology we receive from Jesus in the Gospels is very different. He describes a loving, living God and emphasizes that God is alive with us on earth. His prayer to the Father (the Lord's Prayer) also gives us an ecology of God's presence here with us on earth as in heaven. Jesus also encourages us not to worry about our earthly existence in Matt 6 and in John 16. Along with not worrying about our earthly existence, we are to seek fruits of abundance and pray for the things that we need. It is a cosmology that celebrates the human/nature relationship that flows from a living God's creation. In Jesus' cosmology, sin comes from individual decisions made from free will rather than being something inherited. This is much like the Hebrew understating that the tree of the knowledge of good and evil in the garden of Eden leads us away from God, while the tree of life leads us towards God. This understanding of sin as the choice of the individual is why we do not find the concept of original sin in the Jewish faith.[4]

The cosmology that Jesus presents of the way the universe is ordered has God as living and loving, heaven on earth, and sin as an individual action or choice. This is a completely different cosmology from that of Augustine or the writer of the book of Revelation. And, for an effective understanding of Christian spiritual ecology (CSE), it is important to separate these cosmologies in order to practice this human/nature relationship. This understanding also aligns us with the current state of historical and scientific research, for we will find the science on the benefits of spending time in nature is not in agreement with a cosmology that includes the notion of original sin.

The new field of spiritual ecology is defined by Kara Moses in *The Ecologist* as follows: "Spiritual ecology reunites matter with spirit, with the sacred [*sic*] and brings this into relationship for the needs of our times. The most immediate way we can practice this is in the physicality of our lives."[5] Thus, what is being proposed here in the realm of spiritual ecology is that it is time for us to align our Christian thinking with the scientific and historical research of the contemporary world.

This work looks at scientific research into the benefits for human beings of spending time in nature. This scientific information

4. Ridberg, "Sin and Forgiveness."

5. *The Ecologist*, "Spiritual Ecology."

is then used to support the idea that the ecological relationship is something that should be celebrated and lived out by Christians. The research is preceded by accounts from spiritually minded Christians who describe being spiritually fed when experiencing God and Jesus in the natural world. The research concludes by looking at the possible benefits for the natural world also from living out this ecological relationship.

The sciences tell us that the broken relationship between humanity and the natural world is the greatest contributing factor to global warming and the environmental crisis.[6] Thus the sciences of our times have given us much evidence that it is time for Christians to transcend past doctrines such as that of original sin, which present creation as cursed, and instead develop a spiritual ecological relationship that aligns itself with the Gospels, where Jesus is, as Peter puts it in Matt 16, the son of the living God. That is, it is time to develop a relationship with the living God of creation and with Jesus as the son of creation itself. In John 8, Jesus is identified as the light of the world, with "world" understood in the original Greek meaning of "cosmos." This is very different from the understanding of a created cosmos cursed through original sin. We have been led to believe that the notion of a cursed created cosmos was the Judaic understanding and therefore also Jesus' understanding of the Genesis text. However, in Judaism there is no such an idea of the cosmos, for it was added by Augustine.[7] For this reason, as a rabbi, Jesus would not have envisioned creation as cursed. Therefore, this work is aimed at returning us to the message from the Gospels, while at the same time moving us into the future with a Christian spiritual ecology. This then brings us to the understanding that, by developing our ecological relationship with the natural world, we will be living out a spiritual life with God and Jesus, which is a relationship that is greatly neglected in our contemporary world.

6. NASA, "Causes of Climate Change."

7. Jewish Virtual Library, "Issues in Jewish Ethics"; Yeshiva.co, "Original Sin in Judaism."

THE DEFINITION OF ECOLOGY

Because this book takes an ecological approach, there is a need to provide a foundation for the ecological dialogue. We can begin with a definition of ecology from the Ecological Society of America: "Ecology is the study of relationships between living organisms, including humans, and their physical environment; it seeks to understand the vital connections between plant and animals and the world around them. Ecology also provides information on the benefits of ecosystems and how we can use Earth's resources in ways that leave the environment healthy for future generations."[8] In this work, the particular ecological relationship that is in focus is the human/nature relationship.

Alexander Von Humboldt (1769–1859), who was a naturalist, explorer, and geographer, is considered one of the first ecologists and environmentalists. Von Humboldt's writings influenced thinkers such as Muir, Thoreau, Whitman, and Emerson. As modernity and the Enlightenment were unfolding (which led to our current secularized times), Western Europeans were exploring the earth. The dominant Westernization of the world would create the common perception of nature as a material that could be used by the more intelligent humanity through its development of technology and sciences.[9] Witnessing this transition, Von Humboldt proposed a harmony within nature and the possibility of a spiritual self-awareness through which humanity might realize an eternal God in that relationship. He wrote in *Views of Nature*:

> He who seeks spiritual peace amidst the unresolved strife between peoples therefore gladly lowers his gaze to the quiet life of plants and into the inner workings of the sacred force of nature, or, surrendering to the instinctive drive that has glowed for millennia in the breast of humanity, he look upward with awe to the high celestial

8. Ecological Society of America, "What Is Ecology?"
9. Duke University Press, "Removed from Nature."

> bodies, which, in undisturbed harmony, complete their ancient, eternal course.[10]

It is noteworthy that Von Humboldt, himself an explorer, realized the impact of Westernization by visiting cultures that lived at one with nature and their god(s), much as the early Christians did. Perhaps at that moment there began awareness of the need to discuss our particular humanity/nature ecological relationship.

After Von Humboldt, process theology took the lead in the Christian approach to ecology. Beginning with Alfred North Whitehead, who then influenced John B. Cobb, the idea developed that through our processes of interaction with one another and with nature, we create our reality, which Whitehead termed a "process of concrescence" and "transcendent creativity."[11] If one believes in God as Creator through a process of interaction, we are then in the process of relating to God. The idea of process theology is thus similar to the Christian idea of an ecological relationship. Envisioning this path into ecology, John B. Cobb wrote *Is It Too Late? A Theology of Ecology*, in which he suggests that this ecological approach is something that requires a fresh new look at the relational aspect of ecology, which in turn will lead to changed ways of life:

> But the question remains whether all this will lead only to a series of ad hoc measures designed to meet particular emergencies when public opinion demands it or whether it will lead to careful planning and rethinking of our national life. The latter can occur only if a new vision of humanity and our place in relation to nature comes into being, a vision that would naturally express itself in a changed style of life.[12]

In other words, taking an ecological approach is to literally look at how we live. These spiritual and life aspects of ecology will

10. Von Humboldt, *Views of Nature*, 58.

11. Whitehead, *Process and Reality*, 87.

12. Cobb Jr., *Is It Too Late?*, 14.

be explored in the forthcoming literature review on Christian nature spirituality.

There is a self-awareness that arises when we meditate about how we are living our lives in relation to other things. The realization that as humans we are a part of nature was termed "deep ecology" by the philosopher Arne Naess in 1972. Although the term "deep ecology" originates with Naess, the thinking behind it was influenced by Gandhi's approach to the human/nature relationship. In an article entitled "Nature and Man: The Gandhian Concept of Deep Ecology," Poonam Kumaria writes, "With the attainment of Moksha or self-realization, living being is intimately connected to nature. The intimacy follows the capacity of identification and practice of nonviolence or ahimsa. To quote Gandhi, 'The rock bottom technique for achieving the power of nonviolence is belief in the essential oneness of life.'"[13]

This term "deep ecology" is now widely used in works on ecology and spiritual life. For this work, let it be noted that the understanding of the term is similar to the original concept of Gandhi, in which he highlights the self-realization of our connection to nature. This concept from Gandhi was then radicalized by Naess, who identified eight fundamental values of deep ecology in ways that suggest it transcends religion and should become a guiding principle in society. However, in my view, one takes away from the nonviolent, loving aspect of the ecological relationship if one seeks to impose it on a whole society, or on other individuals, something that will be discussed later in relation to the inclusivity of this ecology. The point here for Christians is that the ecological relationship Cobb saw as awareness leads to an awakening about how we are related to the natural world. This is something he terms "inclusiveness." Cobb writes: "Exclusionists view humanity as outside of nature and in opposition to it. Inclusionists see humanity as within and part of nature."[14] This simple inclusive perspective is akin to Gandhi describing the ecological relationship as "oneness." Such inclusiveness of other cultures and perspectives enables not

13. Kumaria, "Nature and Man."

14. Cobb, *Is It Too Late?*, 63.

only Christians to have this perspective, but any other religious or nonreligious group also. Here again this prevents us from any radicalization of the ecological relationship. Individualizing this relationship also goes against the idea that this relationship is about the interdependence of ourselves, the natural world, and the rest of humanity, as defined by Cobb: "To know myself as within nature is to know that the ecological system of interpenetration and interdependence includes me, both my body and my personality. It is not to cease to think of myself as an individual person, but it is to cease to think of a person as existing prior to or independently of relations. These relations extend throughout the body and throughout the wider environment."[15]

I conclude this discussion by defining the human/nature ecological relationship as one that entails the self-realization of our interdependence with the natural world, which in turn creates inclusivity in that relationship of oneness. I avoid asserting any fundamental values about this relationship, because this would take away its very character of inclusivity, and people should instead feel free to explore this awareness in their own religious and cultural contexts.

By adhering to Gandhi's original concept about the ecological relationship, along with the inclusivity advocated by Cobb, Christians can gain the ability to then speak of their own spiritual ecological relationships along with guidance from Jesus and the Gospels. Jesus' greatest commandment to love God (or the natural world as God's creation), self (through the self-realization of our interconnectedness to nature), and neighbor (by respecting our interconnectedness) thus encapsulates this ecological relationship for Christians. This assertion leads into a review of the lives and works of past Christians who have practiced this kind of spiritual ecological relationship.

15. Cobb, *Is It Too Late?*, 68.

Chapter 2: Forerunners of the Christian Spirituality of Nature

> Jesus answered, "Very truly I tell you, no one can enter the kingdom of God unless they are born of water and the Spirit. Flesh gives birth to flesh, but the Spirit gives birth to spirit. You should not be surprised at my saying, 'You must be born again.' The wind blows wherever it pleases. You hear its sound, but you cannot tell where it comes from or where it is going. So it is with everyone born of the Spirit." (John 3:5–8)

Before looking into scientific research in support of the ecological human/nature relationship, it is worth noting that this relationship has been lived out in practice by various notable Christians as a form of spirituality. In exploring the essence of this relationship, it is interesting to note that none of these spiritual Christians ever incorporated their Christian passion for the natural world into a theology as a set of systematic beliefs. For example, Howard Thurman would never refer to himself as a theologian: "Theologians are too often interested in reducing religion to belief or worse systems of belief. Thurman was a mystic, not a theologian. He begins and ends with experience."[1] Rather than speculate why that is so, it is more important to highlight that these individuals felt their relationship with nature was an important means of enriching their spiritual lives as Christians. Nature was the place to worship God.

1. Open Horizons, "Need for the Mystical."

To look into how this practice might work for Christians, it is important to lay out the framework of the ecological relationship to show why this concept is more about relationship than it is about theology.

Next, from the perspective of tradition, we will look at one traditional resource that has been used in Christianity to speak about the spiritual relationship with God in nature. Celtic Christianity in the traditional sense held fast to the idea of relating with God and Jesus in nature, along with its own struggle with aspects of Christian thought, such as the concept of original sin, which transforms the relationship between humanity and nature into something flawed.

HOWARD THURMAN AND SELF-REALIZATION

A natural place to begin any literature review of a Christian spirituality of nature is with the influential spiritual writer Howard Thurman (1899–1981), who himself visited Gandhi and echoed that leader's belief in the interconnectedness of the human being and the rest of nature. The interconnectedness Thurman refers to as a "common consciousness" is described in a book entitled *What Makes You Come Alive* by Lerita Coleman Brown: "Howard Thurman felt that there was a knowingness—what he called 'common consciousness'—that we could access in nature. We are connected to this common consciousness, yet our awareness of it may remain dormant or underdeveloped."[2] Following the lines of the awakening awareness of Gandhi's deep ecology, Thurman writes that "nature is a balm for the soul that seeks reconciliation and wholeness. Seeing manifestations of sacred unity everywhere is a powerful gift we can receive whenever we go outside."[3] Here Thurman is providing a path towards the beneficial aspect of the human/nature relationship which he describes as "balm for the soul."

2. Brown, *What Makes You Come Alive*, 57.

3. Brown, *What Makes You Come Alive*, 60.

Interestingly, this deep ecology, which Gandhi calls "*ahimsa*,"[4] is an understanding that Thurman gained from his visit with Gandhi.

Even though the term "deep ecology" is actually credited to Arne Naess, when one thinks of Thurman's influence on the civil rights movement and his advocacy of nonviolence, it is evident he was the first to fully adopt this understanding and put it into practice in Western culture. Further detail on the Thurman-Gandhi meeting is provided in *Visions of a Better World*, a book about that meeting during which this concept of *ahimsa* was taught to Thurman: "Thurman, always at his religious core a nature mystic, a romantic vitalist in the mode of Olive Schreiner, was very sympathetic to Gandhi's broader point that the ultimate truth, whether it was labeled God or ahimsa, was at once natural and supernatural, profoundly alive but not limited to any specific living thing. 'If the source of life is alive, then it follows that life itself is alive,' Thurman would write, somewhat cryptically but characteristically, in 1944."

What he meant by this is that there is an underlying moral order in the universe. "The cosmos is the kind of order that sustains and supports the demands that the relationships between men and between man and God be ones of harmony [and] integration." In sum, Gandhi's *ahimsa* was a close relative of Thurman's increasingly unconventional notion of God.[5]

In affirming Cobb's awareness of the inclusivity of the ecological relationship, Thurman also speaks of the teaching of diversity that derives from the relationship. Brown explains: "Diversity is written into nature, and that includes humanity itself. The natural world contributed to the absolute clarity of Thurman's conviction that segregation and discrimination of any kind are unnatural. Such human-imposed divisions are a denial of God, who is the Creator and Author of all life."[6] Once again the theme is of a living God found in the natural universe.

This theme, i.e., that the relationship with nature is interdependent and inclusive, is developed by Thurman, who then

4. Dixie and Eisenstadt, "When Howard Thurman Met Mahatma Gandhi."

5. Dixie and Eisenstadt, "When Howard Thurman Met Mahatma Gandhi."

6. Brown, *What Makes You Come Alive*, 59.

presents Christian ecology as a site of spiritual revelation. The place we experience the divine and eternity spiritually is our place of connection to a living God, which is something Jesus often points to in his own worship. We hear of this connection in a quote from Thurman about his early childhood experience of nature: "The ocean and night together surrounded my little life with the reassurance that could not be affronted by the behavior of human beings," he writes. "The ocean at night gave me a sense of timelessness, of existing beyond the reach of the ebb and flow of circumstances. . . . The experience of these storms gave me a certain overriding immunity against much of the pain I would have to deal with in the years ahead when the ocean was only a memory. The sense held, I felt rooted in life, in nature, in existence."[7] To this ecological understanding, which I have been ascribing to the human/nature relationship, deep ecology, *ahimsa*, and the living God (which Thurman envisions also in his writings), can now be added the Christian understanding of the way Jesus describes himself as spirit and life. This is Thurman's understanding of the ecological relationship with nature.

What is happening in the search for an ecological relationship for Christians is that Thurman is giving a gift to support that journey. However, arising in the past and continuing today in theological discussions about nature and the environment is the discussion of original sin, a doctrine which, as noted, leaves creation cursed and humanity corrupt. From this flows an accompanying difficulty in describing ecological interconnectedness. Writing as a Christian, Thurman actually says the opposite: nature is not only where one can find God, but is also the site of that self-realization Gandhi spoke of as a natural innate quality we are born with. "For Thurman, inner authority, as an innate quality, releases us from mental subjugation and dominance. If another person's words and actions disrupt our peace or composure, they possess the power. We enable them to prevail over our inner life and sense of reality."[8] In this way Thurman frees us from the need to align the Christian

7. Brown, *What Makes You Come Alive*, 44.

8. Brown, *What Makes You Come Alive*, 140.

ecological relationship with current or past thinking about original sin and the idea that creation is cursed. He is saying people are to free themselves from the idea that nature is cursed and instead find themselves within nature. This is the freedom Cobb calls for in his *Theology of Ecology*: a changed style of life.

JOHN MUIR AND SELF-REALIZATION

In the Genesis account of creation in the Bible, God breathes spirit into clay and creates human life. In both Hebrew and Greek the word for "spirit" is synonymous with wind or breath. In Hebrew we find *roo'ach*, meaning "wind," "spirit," "breeze," "life." In Greek it is *pneuma*, meaning "breath of life" and "spirit." Thus, when I talk about spirituality in this review, I am looking at how these past Christians literally breathed their meditation on God and Jesus into their lives, or in simple terms, how they lived their lives. As found with Thurman, spirituality is not only about the way a person lives, but also about the way that person interacts with God and Jesus. The same is true of the environmentalist John Muir (1838–1914). As a young child, Muir had all of the New Testament and most of the Old Testament memorized. While this memorization was from the strict ruling of his Christian father, who would punish Muir if he did not follow his direction, Muir was not dissuaded from Christianity. During his time at the University of Wisconsin, and under the guidance of his lifelong friend Jeanne Carr, Muir learned about a loving God who also aligned with his passion for nature:

> Muir's exposure to geology and botany brought him face to face with science which could not be harmonized with a literal reading of the Bible, but exposure to liberal Christianity showed him a way to reconcile religion and science. Carr's wife, Jeanne, introduced him to the thought of William Ellery Channing, with his positive view of a loving God and indwelling divinity. Muir also

> accepted Agassiz's precept that "a physical fact is as sacred as a moral principle."[9]

As with Thurman, we can begin to see for Muir the infusion of the divinity of God within nature.

The furthering of Muir's dedication to Christianity occurred while he was working as a machinist, and when he had an accident and temporarily lost his sight. During this dark time of blindness and as he began to regain his sight, Muir went through a spiritual conversion and committed his life to studying God's natural creation:

> As soon as I got out into Heaven's light I started on another long excursion, making haste with all my heart to store my mind with the Lord's beauty and thus be ready to any fate, light or dark. And it was from this time that my long continuous wanderings may be said to have fairly commenced. I bade adieu to all my mechanical inventions, determined to devote the rest of my life to the study of the inventions of God.[10]

During this time Muir was influenced by the writings of Alexander Von Humboldt, mentioned above, and came to believe "that one's emotions and subjective views were necessary in order to completely experience nature."[11] This may resonate for us with the concept of self-awareness found in nature from Gandhi and Thurman. Muir did as he said he would do. As part of his dedication to the "inventions of God," he eventually settled in the Sierra Nevada mountains where he worked as a shepherd and wrote about his spiritual experiences in nature.

What Muir does for us on this journey is to poetically describe the self-realization of God in nature and the ecological relationship. The discussion has already moved from defining this self-realization as the essential oneness of being to Thurman's rooted description of eternal timelessness that humans are born

9. Stoll, "God and John Muir."

10. Stoll, "God and John Muir."

11. Byrnes, "Alexander Von Humboldt."

with and innately possess. Now Muir gives a detailed description of being literally baptized and transformed in his self by his natural surroundings. As Muir entered this remote part of the mountains, he began to describe this holy setting in a letter to his friend and mentor Jeanne Carr in this way: "I was in the glorious Yosemite . . . that you would see it, and worship there. . . . It is by far the grandest of all the special temples of nature I was ever permitted to enter. It must be the sanctum of the Sierras, and I trust that you will all be led to it."[12] In another letter to Carr, Muir describes his baptism:

> Never shall I forget my baptism in this font. It happened in January, the resurrection day for many a plant and for me. I suddenly found myself on one of its hills; the hollow overflowed with light, as a fountain, and only small, sunless nooks were kept for mosseries and ferneries. Hollow Creek spangled and mazed like a river. The ground steamed with fragrance. Light, of unspeakable richness, was brooding the flowers. . . . To lovers of the wild, these mountains are not one hundred miles away. Their spiritual power and the goodness of the sky make them here, as a circle of friends. They rise as a portion of the hilled walls of the hollow. You cannot feel yourself out-of-doors; plain, sky, and mountains ray beauty which you feel. You bathe in these spirit-beams, turning round and round, as if warming at a campfire. Presently you lose consciousness of your own separate existence: you blend with the landscape and become part and parcel of nature.[13]

These words take the reader into the midst of a literal description of ecological self-realization. Jeanne Carr, realizing her friend's experience and writing were truly special, encouraged him to share them with society. Muir finished describing his actual conversion/baptism that spring in another letter written to Carr in June:

12. Flinders, *John Muir*, 22.

13. Flinders, *John Muir*, 25–26.

> How glorious a conversion, so complete and wholesome is it. . . . We rather seem to have been so always. Nature like a fluid seems to drench and steep us throughout, as the whole sky and the rocks and flowers are drenched with spiritual life—with God. Now I am not longer a shepherd with a few bruised beans and crackers in my stomach and wrapped in a woolen blanket, but a free bit of everything, not to be defined as to extent nor cramped or bound as to movements more than clouds are.[14]

More of Muir's writings can be found in the book *John Muir: Spiritual Writings*, in which he describes his time in the mountains as an "eternal gift" and "a thousand windows to show us God."

At this point in the journey into Christian spiritual ecology we have come full circle, transitioning from a definition of spiritual ecology to the spiritual ecological relationship described above by Muir. Muir gives us an "amen" in his description, agreeing with Thurman that the eternal conversion in nature is beyond our particular life circumstances. The discussion has thus moved past theory to the point where the oneness or realization of self is the spiritual practice of this ecology. It is a way of life in communion with the living God from Scripture. This aspect of self-realization will be explored more fully in the discussion on the benefits of spending time in nature, along with the idea that doing so heals humanity.

It is my intention in this work to position Christianity and the ecological relationship with nature in alignment with the scientific research of our times. As Thurman noted and instructed, the task is to realize our innate quality, i.e., the self-realization of the ecological relationship. As a movement, the followers of Celtic Christianity lived out that innate quality, and so now I now turn in the final section of this review of the Christian spirituality of nature to discover what lessons on ecology can be learned from the Celts.

14. Flinders, *John Muir*, 26–27.

CELTIC CHRISTIANITY

I believe Celtic Christianity can offer from the Christian tradition an answer to the call from Cobb for "a new vision of humanity in relation to nature."[15] While Thurman and Muir gave us examples of a spiritual ecological life, there is still a need for the definition from a Christian tradition that reflects fully the nature of that relationship, or a firm new belief in the oneness of humanity and nature in contrast to past dualistic Christian thinking.

In his introduction to *Christ of the Celts: The Healing of Creation*, Philip Newell notes that Celtic Christianity asks the question: "Who is Christ for us now?"[16] In other words, are we willing to let go of past beliefs about humanity and nature that may have been mistaken? Concerning a sense of oneness and relationship, he then writes, "To see Christ as leading us further into the unity of life is a belief that was cherished in the ancient Celtic world."[17] The concept of ecological relationship I have been building on this journey is once again the central theme here: "All the great spiritual traditions of humanity have pointed in their distinct ways to the Oneness from which we come and the Oneness that we long for. The Celtic tradition has done this through its love of Christ. He is viewed as leading us not into a separation from the world and the rest of humanity but into a renewed relationship with the Ground of Life, the One from whom all things come."[18]

In the first chapter of Newell's work, titled "Memory of a Song," we are introduced to the idea that we have always had this ecological relationship with nature, but that it is like a song we have forgotten how to sing and play. From an idea about how we are born with this ecological relationship within us as the image of God, Newell writes, "The image of God is the essence of our being. It is the core of the human soul. We are sacred not because we have been baptized or because we belong to one faith tradition over

15. Cobb, *Is It Too Late?*, 14.

16. Newell, *Christ of the Celts*, 6.

17. Newell, *Christ of the Celts*, 8.

18. Newell, *Christ of the Celts*, 8.

another. We are sacred because we have been born."[19] This would also mean the garden of Eden is a place of lost human identity. "Deep within us is a longing for union, for our genesis is in the One from whom all things have come. Our home is the Garden, and deep within us is the yearning to hear its song again."[20]

The roots of Celtic Christianity are in the traditions deriving from Jesus' disciple John, which he passed on to his own disciples, including Irenaeus. From the Secret Book of John and the Gospel of Thomas, along with other accounts of John witnessing to Jesus after his resurrection, Newell writes, "Christ says to John, in this brief account, that humanity has forgotten itself. We suffer from a 'bond of forgetfulness,' he says. We do not know ourselves nor do we remember our beginnings. We are in what is like a deep sleep. And the more distant we become from our true self, the more we fall under the sway of the false self, or what he calls 'the counterfeit spirit.'"[21] When one recalls that in Hebrew thought there was an understanding that the Messiah was to signify the return of Adam, this encounter between John and the resurrection of Jesus really begins to make sense. As we know from Scripture, Jesus is described as the "Author of Life," which is a term for Jesus that Thurman also uses in his description of the ecological relationship.

Jesus as the "Author of Life" helps us remember our natural selves as truly natural, as described by Newell: "Christ is often referred to in the Celtic tradition as the truly natural one. He comes not to make us more than natural or somehow other than natural but to make us truly natural. He comes to restore us to the original root of our being. As the twentieth-century French mystic-scientist Teilhard de Chardin says much later in the Celtic world, grace is 'the seed of resurrection' sown in our nature. It is given not to make us something other than ourselves but to make us radically ourselves."[22] This description here sounds very similar to the understanding of oneness from Gandhi and the term later

19. Newell, *Christ of the Celts*, 17.

20. Newell, *Christ of the Celts*, 18.

21. Newell, *Christ of the Celts*, 19.

22. Newell, *Christ of the Celts*, 22.

given to it of "deep ecology." As Thurman puts it, "the source of all life is alive,"[23] which is affirmed by the Celtic tradition in talking about the same Christian spiritual ecological relationship.

This idea that the human/nature relationship is the source of our life will be explored in the following chapter on the physical and mental health benefits of the relationship with nature under the scientific term "biophilia." Interestingly, this concept of biophilia is already to be found within the Celtic tradition in the remembrance of our natural relationship with this source or with the truly natural one. It is an aspect of human existence that we have forgotten. Newell writes as follows:

> Alexander Scott, the nineteenth-century Celtic teacher, uses the analogy of a plant suffering from blight. If such a plant were shown to botanists, even if the botanists had never seen that type of plant before, they would define it in terms of its essential life features. They would identify the plant with reference to its healthy properties of height and color and scent. They would not define it in terms of its blight. Rather they would say that the blight is foreign to the plant, that it is attacking the essence of the plant. Now this may seem a very obvious botanical point. But maybe it is so obvious that we have missed the point when it comes to defining human nature. We have tended to define ourselves and one another in terms of the blight, in terms of sin or evil, in terms of the failings or illnesses of our lives, instead of seeing what is deeper still, the beauty of the image of God at the core of our being.[24]

The biophilia concept is also reflected in the idea that our human bodies have a need to relate to the rest of nature, as it is part of our biological existence. If we recall Muir's baptism in the mountains and his relational ecological experience, we are now able to define these experiences as Christian, in that he was experiencing his human self, remembering its core essential connection to God and the natural world. All the research thus far is talking

23. Dixie and Eisenstadt, "When Howard Thurman Met Mahatma Gandhi."

24. Newell, *Christ of the Celts*, 23.

about the same ecological relationship. Newell finishes his section on remembering this forgotten tune by identifying it with the light coming into the world, as described in the Gospel of John.

In order for us as Christians to remember this song of oneness of the ecological relationship, we need to untangle the doctrine of original sin, because this idea of Jesus as the Author of Life and light in the world is snuffed out in the concept of original sin. As Newell explains:

> If a child grows up being told she is ugly or stupid or selfish, at some level she comes to believe that about herself. The descriptions haunt her self-understanding and she lives in a state of doubt about her deepest identity. This is exactly what has happened in relation to the doctrine of original sin, a belief that has dominated the landscape of Western Christian thought and practice since the fourth century. It teaches that what is deepest in us is opposed to God rather than of God. It means that we are essentially ignorant rather than bearers of light.[25]

For Celtic Christians in particular, this doctrine of original sin never made sense because of their belief in the human/nature relationship. Pelagius from Wales is one such person who foresaw the consequences of the doctrine in the fourth century. It was a realization that led him to oppose it with all his strength. "His concern was that if the Church defined the human soul as essentially sinful, it would undermine us in our journey toward wholeness."[26] As Christians, we tend to think that because this doctrine has been around so long it is in the Gospels. However, the truth is Jesus never advocated the doctrine, and it was only added to Christianity hundreds of years later. Says Newell: "The doctrine of original sin was a convenient 'truth' for the builders of empire. They could continue to conquer the world and subdue peoples. And now they could do it with the authority of a divine calling."[27]

25. Newell, *Christ of the Celts*, 28.
26. Newell, *Christ of the Celts*, 28.
27. Newell, *Christ of the Celts*, 29.

Staying true to the Celtic tradition and its early appearance in the teachings of the disciple John, Newell refers to Irenaeus, who was taught by Polycarp, an actual disciple of John's.

> Irenaeus uses a term that at first sight seems complicated. He speaks of Christ as "recapitulating" creation. What do we do when we recapitulate something? We say it again. We repeat something that has already been said but in a way that brings into focus the essence of what was previously said but has been forgotten or obscured. Irenaeus teaches that Christ expresses the heart of the first work of God, namely the work of creation, the deepest and most essential energy of the Creator.[28]

Here again we find the opposite of the concept of original sin proposed by Augustine, who did not himself have a direct discipleship connection to John and Jesus as Irenaeus did.

I am able to write this work from my standing of ordination in the UCC Church without concern, with encouragement, in fact, as my particular tradition is non-credal. I am also encouraged by my belief in Jesus to continue writing according to my own personal faith journey. This is termed as the "God is still speaking" understanding in my tradition. However, it is important to recall, while exploring the Celtic tradition and its timeless belief in the human/nature relationship, that in an ecumenical sense we have thus far heard from many traditions: Cobb as a Methodist, Thurman as a Baptist, Muir as an Evangelical, and now the Celtic tradition as a whole. I thus believe this spiritual ecology can be practiced within any Christian tradition. What is different in this work is that I am looking to create a spiritual ecology for Christians that can be practiced with reference to the research into, and scientific evidence of the benefits of the human/nature ecological relationship. For Christians, a common sense and matter-of-fact

28. Newell, *Christ of the Celts*, 43.

approach can then be adopted in the practice of the relationship. This is the reason this journey begins with John Cobb's call for a new way of life for Christians, or in Thurman's words, with finding this "innate quality," and in so doing, release ourselves "from mental subjugation."

It is time start a new chapter in Christianity, time to remember this forgotten song of our ecological relationship with nature. In *Celtic Christianity: Deep Roots for a Modern Faith*, the author, Ray Simpson, poetically describes the process entailed in this work:

> Celtic spirituality resonates with leaders of House Churches and other denominations. One House Church leader happened to hear some worship led by musicians of the Northumbria Community at a gathering for northern church leaders at Bradford Cathedral. Although he had no place for liturgy in his tradition, this Celtic worship reduced him to tears. He determined to find out what it was that had touched him so deeply, and so he drove over 300 miles to meet members of the Northumbria Community who had been invited to my cottage at Lindisfarne. This man was always active, totally committed, a church planter. He read aloud some words pinned on to a book-end about there being a contemplative in all of us, and he began to weep; a new dimension of God was overwhelming him. He asked what it meant. Someone suggested that he represented one of many fresh streams of spiritual life flowing in the nation; these streams were recent and on the surface. Yet unknown to many, a much older stream had always been flowing underground, deep and pure. Now it was coming nearer the surface and these other streams were to cross it and even to flow together for part of their way.[29]

In this sense then, from the above example from the Celtic tradition, we are simply making space in Christian practice to have the language and resources to speak of the human/nature ecology as Christians.

29. Simpson, *Celtic Christianity*, 46.

CONCLUSION

The focus of this review has been on the practice of the ecological relationship as a way of life or a form of spirituality. My purpose was to ask what it looks like to live in the ecological idea of oneness with nature, as proposed in the first section on defining ecology. Before us we have some fine examples from Thurman, Muir, and the Celts, all of whom shared a belief as Christians that the relationship with nature is a way of relating spiritually to God and Jesus. In the sense of spirit, wind, and breath, this is how they lived their lives.

What is even more profound than their example demonstrating that this ecological relationship is practical and beneficial for Christians is that the influence arising from their natural spirituality had an effect on the world. Thurman, as we know, had profound impact on the civil rights movement and his work continues to inspire people in our current times. Muir camped out with President Woodrow Wilson in the Sierra Nevadas and that experience changed Wilson's life and led to the creation of United States National Parks system, which to this day is a great feat of ecological preservation. In essence, as Jesus explained when his disciples had broken the law, what is actually defiling is what is in someone's heart. The verse that he quotes from Isaiah is that they "honor me with their lips, but their hearts are far from me" (Isa 29:13; also found in Matt 15:8–9; Mark 7:6–7). I believe here Jesus is explaining that what matters is our example and how we live our lives in spirit, along with his additional law to love one another in the way he has loved us. And so these examples not only teach us it is good to live in that ecological relationship, but that the spiritual practice of that relationship can be an inspiration and a source of healing for the world.

We have moved from a definition of the ecological relationship to its spiritual practice as Christians and finished with a vision of this practice from the teachings of the Celtic tradition. The gift from the Celtic tradition in this dialogue is like the gift from the spiritual teachers Muir and Thurman, in that it too offers the go-ahead, or the affirmation that it is good to practice the relationship with nature. The Celtic tradition offers to all Christians a historical root in that lost song the disciples learned from John. It is not only acceptable to practice that relationship, but it is also a practice that is aligned with the Gospels and with Jesus as the Author of Life and the light of the natural world.

This work is in the form of a model of ministry. In this form I have made the case through the research on ecology that a Christian spirituality of nature, a Christian ecology, is both practical and inspiring. Therefore, from the Christian perspective of ministry, it is something that should be advocated, taught, and preached about, and this will be covered later in the book. Before I do that and this model of ministry becomes clearer, we will solidify it with scientific research on the benefits of the human/nature ecological relationship.

Chapter 3: Scientific Research on the Benefits of Being in Nature

> "Do not come any closer," God said. "Take off your sandals, for the place where you are standing is holy ground." (Exodus 3:5)

The purpose of this chapter is to revisit the practice of an ecological relationship with nature and back it with evidence from scientific research. The reason for doing so stems from my belief that this is necessary for us as Christians living in the contemporary secularized world. We are in a time beyond the Enlightenment, a time when as a secular society we trust scientific information above any belief system. This is unlikely to change. If we were to take examples of all the healing benefits of nature discovered during research solely from the medical field, it is highly likely that we would find ways to harmonize that scientific research with our belief systems.

What I propose then aligns Christians with the contemporary world. It lets us fact-check our beliefs in this matter against the scientific research. Thus, when considering cosmological research, which is the study of how the universe is composed, we are reminded that past beliefs we may hold on to as Christians are largely based on past outdated scientific research. One example of this which still has impact for an understanding of the human/

nature relationship comes from Aristotle and his Ptolemaic model.[1] Aristotle's scientific beliefs about the makeup of the universe were adopted by theologians such as Augustine all the way through to Martin Luther. In this model, the earth and not the sun is the center of the universe. It is from Aristotle that we also get the concept of the great chain of being, and the idea that humans, in the sense of a cosmological order, are more intelligent than other parts of the natural world, a concept known as *Scala Naturae*. If this is our understanding of the human/nature relationship, its impact on the world is as Lori Marino describes:

> As long as we view ourselves as "higher than" or "qualitatively different from" the other animals, we will continue to make assumptions about them that promote abuse and exploitation. The Scala Naturae gives us license to exploit other animals because they are seen as being further down the ladder. It also helps us to view ourselves as not being fully part of nature, and therefore to disconnect from empathizing with other animals. It seems to give us a "right" to treat them as commodities for our own use. Even seemingly well-intentioned ideas about stewardship and dominion are ultimately just manifestations of the same hierarchical view that leads to abuse and exploitation.[2]

The point here is that our Christian ecology/theology has an effect on how we relate to one another and the natural world. Obviously, these concepts are now outdated in light of the advancement of our sciences, which gives point to the need to create a new ecology that is in line with current scientific thinking.

It is as if we are trying to go around in vehicles with square tires because we have been told they need to be square. For this reason, the next part of this exploratory journey looks into scientific research in relation to the proposed Christian spiritual ecology: the idea that we as humans should live a life of oneness with

1. Vainio, *Cosmology in Theological Perspective*, 23.
2. Marino, "Scala Naturae Is Alive and Well."

the natural world to better understand ourselves and God through a relationship with Jesus, the Author of Life.

BIOPHILIA

This section of the chapter concerns O. E. Wilson's biophilia hypothesis. In the prologue of *Biophilia: The Human Bond with Other Species*, Wilson writes as follows as a way of introducing us to his biological theory:

> I will make the case that to explore and affiliate with life is a deep and complicated process in mental development. To an extent still undervalued in philosophy and religion, our existence depends on this propensity, our spirit is woven from it, hope rises on its currents. There is more. Modern biology has produced a genuinely new way of looking at the world that is incidentally congenial to the inner direction of biophilia. In other words, instinct is in this rare instance aligned with reason. The conclusion I draw is optimistic: to the degree that we come to understand other organisms, we will place a greater value on them, and on ourselves.[3]

One might pause here for a moment and reflect on how similar this sounds to Gandhi and his understanding of self-realization.

The end of Wilson's first chapter describes, from a biologist's point of view, the multitudinous explorations of biological species in the world. He outlines the mass of information provided from these explorations and the intelligence they reveal within each biological species. He then puts forward his notion of "biophilia" in contrast to the traditional idea of the great chain of being. "It seems possible that the naturalist's vision is only a specialized product of a biophilic instinct shared by all, that it can be elaborated to benefit more and more people. Humanity is exalted not because we are so far above other living creatures, but because knowing them well elevates the very concept of life."[4] Here, as he develops his

3. Wilson, *Biophilia*, 1–2.

4. Wilson, *Biophilia*, 22.

biophilia hypothesis, it starts to become clear that, like the original thoughts on ecology discussed earlier, biophilia has a lot to do with awareness. In other words, the self-awareness identified by Von Humboldt, the interdependence noted by Cobb, the concept of self-realization from Gandhi, and the common consciousness and sacred unity described by Thurman are now characterized as an instinctive concept of life.

As I begin to make a case for the ecological harmony between humanity and the natural world, Wilson gives the nod to the need for our beliefs and the humanities and sciences to align for the betterment of all: "The distinction between the two cultures of science and the humanities made famous by C. P. Snow thus persists. Until that fundamental divide is closed or at least reconciled in some congenial manner, the relation between man and the living world will remain problematic."[5] To close this gap, Wilson explains his understanding of humans as biological beings.

> We are in the fullest sense a biological species and will find little ultimate meaning apart from the remainder of life. The fiery circle of disciplines will be closed if science looks at the inward journey of the artist's mind, making art and culture objects of study in the biological mode, and if the artist and critic are informed of the workings of the mind and the natural world as illuminated by the scientific method. In principle at least, nothing can be denied to the humanities, nothing to science.[6]

It is on this point that this book looks to offer something new and close the gap between science and the humanities by aligning belief with scientific research.

Wilson goes on to suggest that perhaps this gap is a myth. The gap in the study of science and the prevailing understanding of human biology stem from the theoretical view of Aristotle, i.e., that human intelligence provides great ability to subdue and conquer nature.

5. Wilson, *Biophilia*, 48.
6. Wilson, *Biophilia*, 82.

> The truth is that we never conquered the world, never understood it; we only think we have control. We do not even know why we respond a certain way to other organisms, and need them in diverse ways, so deeply. The prevailing myths concerning our predatory actions toward each other and the environment are obsolete, unreliable, and destructive. The more the mind is fathomed in its own right, as an organ of survival, the greater will be the reverence for life for purely rational reasons.[7]

This myth and understanding is similar to the "counterfeit spirit" from Celtic Christianity identified later in this journey into ecotherapy as a "big lie." And from our Christian perspective, it is like the tree of knowledge that separates us from God and creation, because we have stopped realizing the relationship.

Wilson's biophilia hypothesis goes beyond the belief that there is need for the human/nature relationship to the idea that such a relationship is actually part of our biological makeup as a human species. Wilson uses the word "instinct" much as Thurman uses the word "innate." In other words this biophilia is within our being, something we are born with, the capacity to understand ourselves as a part of the natural world. To close this section, as I move into exploring the application of the biophilia hypotheses, in simple terms the case being made here for the relationship with nature is that "separated completely from the natural world we will find little ultimate meaning apart from the remainder of life." It is for this scientific reason that humanity is a biological species in need of the relationship. And so, while we might almost call it common sense—just as we know we cannot survive without food, water, and sunlight—because of our tendency as humans to overthink and over-theorize, we have developed as a society to basically live beyond common sense, for we have stopped understanding the life-giving aspects of the natural world.

7. Wilson, *Biophilia*, 139.

FOREST BATHING

What I really like about the concept and practice of Japanese "forest bathing" is that it is very approachable in the sense of its inclusiveness. I could write at great length about my experiences of surfing and the relationship with nature that is part of that; however that is not likely to be relatable to non-surfers. Forest bathing, on the other hand, is approachable for most and gives us a chance to explore Wilson's biophilia hypothesis in a practical way. This is not to say the necessity of the human/nature relationship could not be explored in a vast variety of ways. One could demonstrate the human/nature relationship in terms of gardening or food preparation, for example, which will be explored in the conclusion of this work. We might also note that this exploration of the ecological relationship has moved from a definition of belief to a spiritual practice, then on to the scientific definition of the relationship, and now to the healing practice of that relationship.

Qing Li is a scientist and professor at the Nippon Medical School in Tokyo. He takes us into the woods and his explanation of the forest bathing he advocates starts with the biophilia hypothesis from Wilson, which he then advances to say, yes, we are a part of nature:

> We are part of the natural world. Our rhythms are the rhythms of nature. As we walk slowly through the forest, seeing, listening, smelling, tasting and touching, we bring our rhythms into step with nature. Shinrin-yoku is like a bridge. By opening our senses, it bridges the gap between us and the natural world. And when we are in harmony with the natural world we can begin to heal. Our nervous system can reset itself, our bodies and minds can go back to how they ought to be. No longer out of kilter with nature but once again in tune with it, we are refreshed and restored. We may not travel very far on our forest walk but, in connecting us with nature, shinrin-yoku takes us all the way home to our true selves.[8]

8. Li. *Forest Bathing*, 14.

Shinrin is Japanese for "forest" and *yoku* means "bath." Li takes us back to the discussion about how the ecological relationship is an awareness, the self-realization I have been establishing, as he describes our senses.

He goes on to explain that in both religions of Japan, Shinto and Buddhism, the forest is considered the realm of the divine. For Shinto, the belief is that the Kami spirits are one with the woods. As for the reason why one should forest bathe, Qing Li offers the statistic with which I began this book and which will be explored further in the "healing humanity" section: "We are also, increasingly, an indoor species. According to the US Environmental Protection Agency, the average American now spends 93 percent of their time indoors, of which 6 percent is spent in cars. That makes only one half of one day spent outdoors in a week. Europeans fare no better, spending around 90 percent of their time indoors."[9] This point enters the science behind what is going on here. Li writes that increased urbanization and technology use has added anxiety and stress to our lives, which in turn contributes to major health issues: "The more stress we have, the sicker we get. We have more heart attacks, strokes and cancer. And we have more mental illness, more addictions, loneliness, depression and panic attacks. And, of course, the more stress we have, the more expensive our health care becomes. Anxiety and depression cost the EU about 170 billion euros a year. They cost America $210 billion."[10] The World Health Organization (WHO) calls stress the health epidemic of the twenty-first century, he adds. Here he provides a direct scientific reason as to why this indoor generation has the problems in physical and mental health that it does.

Next, he provides the medicine that is the object of this ecological exploration, the self-realization I have been making a case for:

> The good news is that even a small amount of time in nature can have an impact on our health. A two-hour forest bath will help you to unplug from technology and

9. Li, *Forest Bathing*, 33.
10. Li, *Forest Bathing*, 36.

> slow down. It will bring you into the present moment and de-stress and relax you. When you connect to nature through all five of your senses, you begin to draw on the vast array of benefits the natural world provides. There is now a wealth of data that proves that shinrin-yoku can: reduce blood pressure, lower stress, improve cardiovascular and metabolic health, lower blood sugar levels, improve concentration and memory, lift depression, improve pain thresholds, improve energy, boost the immune system with an increase in the count of the body's natural killer (NK) cells, increase anti-cancer protein production, and help you lose weight.[11]

This is, in effect, a medical explanation of John Muir's baptism in the mountains.

In 2004, Qing Li began what may have been the very first empirical scientific research into the benefit of spending time in nature. Up to this point the research was more hypothetical, as in the earlier discussion of self-realization or even the biophilia hypothesis. The forest therapy study group was able to prove through empirical research that forest bathing "lowers the stress hormones cortisol and adrenaline, suppresses the sympathetic or 'flight or fight' system, enhances the parasympathetic 'rest and recover' system, and lowers blood pressure and increases heart rate variability."[12] Forest bathing has now developed into a certified practice in Japan, with sixty-two certified sites and two and a half to five million participants a year.[13] Forest bathing has also been found to help with sleep: "Sleep deficiency is linked to numerous health problems, including increased risk of heart disease, kidney disease, high blood pressure, diabetes and stroke."[14] The results come from testing, which showed a significant increase in sleep time during forest bathing trips, thus "proving that you sleep better

11. Li, *Forest Bathing*, 37.
12. Li, *Forest Bathing*, 66.
13. Li, *Forest Bathing*, 68.
14. Li, *Forest Bathing*, 68.

when you spend time in a forest, even when you don't significantly increase the amount of physical activity you do."[15]

This is only the beginning, as forest bathing has also been found to improve mood through Profile of Mood State testing: "These are, of course, subjective scores, but objective data backs them up. The levels of measurable stress hormones in women fell after forest bathing, which supports the improvement in mood they recorded on their POMS questionnaires."[16] This finding will be explored further in the next section on ecotherapy.

Forest bathing is also found to boost the immune system through increased activity in natural killer (NK) cells. In further scientific research into what is it about the trees themselves that is able have this effect, investigation was made into the effect of phytoncides:

> As well as having a higher concentration of oxygen, the air in the forest is also full of phytoncides. Phytoncides are the natural oils within a plant and are part of a tree's defence system. Trees release phytoncides to protect them from bacteria, insects and fungi. Phyton is Greek for "plant," and cide is "to kill." Phytoncides are also part of the communication pathway between trees: the way trees talk to each other. The concentration of phytoncides in the air depends on the temperature and other changes that take place throughout the year. The warmer it is, the more phytoncides there are in the air. The concentration of phytoncides is at its highest at temperatures of around 30 degrees Celsius.[17]

Phytoncides are taken in through our sense of smell as the terpenes produced by the trees. "Evergreens like pine trees, cedars, spruces and conifers are the largest producers of phytoncides. We will look more at what the forest smells like in the next chapter. For now, it will be enough to explain that the main components of

15. Li, *Forest Bathing*, 69.
16. Li, *Forest Bathing*, 76.
17. Li. *Forest Bathing*, 88.

phytoncides are terpenes, and these are what you can smell when you do shinrin-yoku in the forest."[18]

Through the employment of research into wood and the essential oils of these terpenes, the following findings about these terpenes was that they

> significantly increased the numbers of NK cells and NK activity, as well as enhancing the activity of the anti-cancer proteins Significantly decreased the levels of stress hormones Increased the hours of sleep Decreased the scores for tension/anxiety, anger/hostility and fatigue/confusion. Other researchers have shown that phytoncides can: Stimulate a pleasant mood Significantly lower blood pressure and heart rate Increase heart-rate variability Suppress sympathetic nervous activity and increase parasympathetic nervous activity, bringing your nervous system into balance and making you feel comfortable and relaxed.[19]

Still more benefits of forest bathing have been identified. For example, there is a substance in the soil that we take in when in the forest or gardening. It is called Mycobacterium vaccae, or M-vaccae, and is linked through research to an improved immune system that stimulates our emotions. "In other words, the soil stimulates the immune system, and a boosted immune system makes us feel happy. Every time you dig in your garden or eat a vegetable plucked from the ground, you will be ingesting M. vaccae and giving yourself this boost."[20] Better congenital function is also linked to trees. One study undertaken by the University of Michigan into the effects on memory and attention when engaging with nature found that people could remember 20 percent more "after they had been for a walk where there are trees than when they had walked through busy city streets."[21] Nature can also improve our creativity and problem-solving. "Nature also has the

18. Li. *Forest Bathing*, 89.

19. Li, *Forest Bathing*, 98.

20. Li, *Forest Bathing*, 103.

21. Li, *Forest Bathing*, 104.

power to help us solve problems and to break through creative blocks. Research at the universities of Utah and Kansas looked at the effect on creative reasoning skills of being immersed in nature for a number of days. The researchers concluded that there 'is a real, measurable cognitive advantage to be realized if we spend time truly immersed in a natural setting,' and found that spending time in nature can boost problem-solving ability and creativity by 50 per cent."[22] Nature is also found to have health benefits achieved through our sense of sight, with many studies showing that patients in hospitals who have views of nature through their windows have better health results. "Patients with a 'green' view need less medication and are discharged sooner after surgery than those who don't have a window or whose room looks out on to a wall."[23] Before concluding this section on forest bathing, it can be noted there is substantial scientific evidence prompting us as Christians to practice a Christian spiritual ecology. There is now proof of what Muir and Thurman experienced in self-realization through their relationship with nature.

Essentially, the techniques of forest bathing are about engaging the five senses. In the above research section mention was made of the benefits of smell, taste, and sight, so the question turns to the impact on hearing and touch. Li answers the question about sound by commenting that natural silence is being lost in our current world. "With such high levels of noise everywhere, most people no longer have the opportunity to enjoy the restorative sounds of peace and quiet. Natural silence has been called one of the most endangered resources on the planet."[24] Of the benefits of natural sound he writes as follows:

> Studies have repeatedly shown that we prefer the sounds of nature to the sounds of urban noise, that the sounds of nature relieve stress and that we feel relaxed when we can hear birdsong or running water. Researchers at Brighton and Sussex Medical School (UK) investigating

22. Li, *Forest Bathing*, 106.

23. Li, *Forest Bathing*, 111.

24. Li, *Forest Bathing*, 154.

> the connection between the brain, the body and background noise, looked at what happened in people's brains while they listened to a series of sounds from either natural or man-made environments. . . . While they listened, the participants had to perform a cognitive task. Their heart rates were monitored as well as their nervous systems, blood pressure, metabolism and digestion as they listened. The results showed that when the participants listened to artificial sounds, their attention was focused inwards. Inward-focused attention is associated with worry and brooding. When they listened to the sounds of nature, they turned their attention outwards. In addition, participants did less well on their tests when they were listening to man-made noise. The nature sounds decreased the functioning of the body's sympathetic nervous system ("fight or flight") and increased the parasympathetic system ("rest and recover"), indicating that we are more relaxed when we listen to nature.[25]

While there is no specific research on the benefits of touch, some of the ways to engage the sense of touch include spring baths and the technique of grounding, which means going barefoot or having nonrubber-soled shoes. There is also the practice of earthing, although the research is still relatively new in this field. Li finishes *Forest Bathing* with a number of useful suggestions on how to practice it. For the sake of this work, I will remain focused on the benefits of spending time in nature in the sense of relationship and ecology by moving to a review of the literature on ecotherapy.

ECOTHERAPY

Remaining true to a focus on the healing of the ecological relationship between humanity and the natural world, I have traversed this exploration from the perspective of the self-realization of the relationship, a perspective that was then justified by scientific research into the benefits of the relationship. This section on ecotherapy moves on to explore the relationship between human beings and

25. Li, *Forest Bathing*, 163–64.

nature from the perspective of mental health. While the preceding section focused on the physical and cognitive health benefits of nature, the inquiry now shifts to mental health. It is widely understood that there are rising levels of anxiety and mental health problems especially among the youth of this indoor generation. Here the relationship between nature and humanity becomes a psychological question.

Addressing this question, an article from the APA's *Nurtured by Nature* gives a list of data that supports the idea that spending time in nature improves our cognitive functioning as well our mental health.[26] This information then can be applied in the field of counseling. In the foreword to a collection of essays entitled *Ecotherapy: Healing with Nature in Mind*, David Orr boldly takes on this question, writing, "If we have a connection with nature that expresses itself more authentically as love and loyalty than as guilt and fear, then freeing the ecological unconscious may be the key to sanity in our time."[27] He engages with the ecological relationship right away to suggest that damage to the connection or interdependence with nature is in fact the problem. "Therapists become ecotherapists when we feel this pain and look to nature (both our own human nature as well as the natural world) as a teacher and source of healing; when we see that human suffering is intimately connected with the destruction of the web of life, and that healing is about making deep changes in the way we live and relate to the world around us."[28] What *Ecotherapy* is also suggesting is that the cultural idea of the great chain of being with which this review began is damaging to the natural world and perhaps also damaging to the human psyche. Orr writes as follows:

> When we see humans like cells within the body of the earth, we understand that our physical, emotional, intellectual, and spiritual health depends on the health of our "vast selves." This challenges our current Western notions of self in relation to world, where humans are

26. Weir, *Nurtured by Nature*.
27. Buzzell and Chalquist, *Ecotherapy*, 37.
28. Buzzell and Chalquist, *Ecotherapy*, 38.

> seen to exist on top of a revolving ball of dead matter. Instead, this indigenous concept of self sees humans as inhabiting a larger living body. As ecotherapists we can draw on these perspectives to describe a self that extends beyond our skin—an ecological self that is in the same moment spiritual.[29]

This sounds a lot like Gandhi's deep ecology. A common thread is emerging through this work: ideas about self-realization, a vast self, deep ecology, and biophilia are forming into something we can further define as a spiritual ecological relationship in ways that have not been attempted before. This point is explored further in the discussion of the healing of humanity later in this work.

We find here in the field of ecotherapy the suggestion that because the human/nature relationship is so broken in our times, we are in need of healing that relationship. This means asking what nature needs in the relationship as well. Robert Greenway, a pioneer of ecopsychology, describes ecotherapy (applied or clinical ecopsychology) as the process of "healing the human-nature relationship through connecting and reconnecting with natural processes."[30] Linda Buzzell, the volume's editor, writes: "Restoring people's relationship with the natural world is, in my experience, one of the most exciting, rewarding, and relevant healing practices on Earth today."[31] The idea that will be explored here concerning the healing of the relationship is that there is a twofold restorative benefit in healing this relationship: both humanity and the natural world are impacted.

When applying ecotherapy, we discover and acknowledge that the world we currently live in involves a massive amount of screen time and busy schedules that do not allow the time needed to heal the human/nature relationship, as noted in "The Nature of Americans' National Report." Part of the process then is to ask people to look at their lifestyles and way they are living in relationship to nature: "All these questions are different ways of framing

29. Buzzell and Chalquist, *Ecotherapy*, 45.
30. Buzzell and Chalquist, *Ecotherapy*, 48.
31. Buzzell and Chalquist, *Ecotherapy*, 48–49.

two basic inquiries: Are you living in harmony with nature—your own nature as a human animal and the larger nature that embraces us all? And are your natural needs being met with your current career and lifestyle?" Buzzell records that if a client answers no to either of these questions, she discusses the changes that person might make to improve their life, and also the life of the planet.[32]

Another therapist, Sara Harris, shares her experience of connecting to the harmony of nature in a chapter entitled "Beyond the 'big lie.'" In a work with Meredith Little, entitled *The Four Shields: The Initiatory Seasons of Human Nature*, Steven Foster coined the term "big lie" with reference to the dominant worldview of humanity as separate from nature. The dualism I noted in relation to the doctrine of original sin, the great myth from Celtic Christianity, and the separation narrative from the great chain of being now has another term, "the big lie."

Harris writes about her development as a therapist through continued learning about harmony with nature, and mentions the influence of John Davis, a teacher at Naropa University and the Ridhwan School, and an experienced guide with the School of Lost Borders.

> Writing about how ecology, psychology, and spiritual understanding inform one another, [Davis] proposes that ecopsychology should encompass "a view that both includes and transcends nature-as-family and nature-as-self metaphors, recognizing a fundamentally nondual, seamless unity in which both nature and psyche flow as expressions of the same ground or source. . . . It calls for levels of development beyond the individual self as a separate entity to identification with being, with spirit, or the mystery, which gives rise to all manifestations, human and nature."[33]

Once again, we are encountering the self-realization of biophilia in a way that continues to give credibility to the human/nature relationship.

32. Buzzell and Chalquist, *Ecotherapy*, 53.
33. Buzzell and Chalquist, *Ecotherapy*, 88.

Sara Harris then describes how she applies this self-realization in her own work as a therapist:

> I teach clients about the universal aspects of rites of passage: severance from your usual world, crossing the threshold into sacred time, releasing your old self and opening to something larger, and returning to your life with the new gifts you have been given. There is enactment and engagement with life's dilemmas, rather than just analysis. Feeling opens up. These ways are so simple, but through giving a client a clear way to turn a regular walk into a ceremony, reverence and wonder can emerge. The senses, soul, and heart open, and a more fully awake human can grow.[34]

Her approach here is attuned to the idea explored in my definition of spiritual ecology, i.e., that it is a realization or awareness of the relationship that is needed.

On this continued topic of awakening to ecological self-realization, Sarah Anne Edwards and Linda Buzzell provide a guide through the steps of the process of awakening in their chapter in *Ecotherapy* titled "The Waking-Up Syndrome." For those trained in counseling, these steps may sound similar to the stages in grief counseling. They are denial, semiconsciousness, awakening, shock, despair, and empowerment.[35] The authors conclude with the notion of empowerment and the idea that there are healing and benefits to the relationship and allowing that to guide our awakening.

> At a conference, agricultural activist and feminist Vandana Shiva offered this advice: "We need to wake up to the problems in the world and yet not get overwhelmed by the magnitude of them . . . not suffer in our activism, but instead find joy in what we are doing to help ameliorate the global problems." Such wisdom seems to be the secret to living positively while navigating the painful stages of awakening. We must strive to enjoy the daily

34. Buzzell and Chalquist, *Ecotherapy*, 90.

35. Buzzell and Chalquist, *Ecotherapy*, 124–28.

> challenges our situation poses, using them as a way to express our creativity and our deep and abiding love for our lives on this earth.[36]

The collected work *Ecotherapy: Healing with Nature in Mind* continues with chapters on processes of natural therapy that dive into shamanic, mystical, and dream therapy approaches.

In the context of this discussion on Christian spiritual ecology, these practices are definitely worthy of merit, and at individual levels could be further explored. I personally prefer to keep this work inclusive, in that I have no wish to exclude any individual or culture. The practice of mysticism in my own personal witness is sacred and holy to the individual self. There are as many individual mystical practices as there are individuals in the world. Thus, for me as a Christian to try to define mysticism for another would be limiting. To put it another way, it would be inclusive of me to say I am enriched by my own personalized nature-based diet, exercise routine, and practice of surfing. However, for me to say this is how everyone should live would be noninclusive.

We should each be encouraged to find our own personal definition of mysticism in our own faith tradition and culture. I have learned this teaching in my own Christian faith. The fact that we all have personal relationships with Jesus means that there are as many versions of Christianity as there are individual Christians in the world. This is an idea which is explored in a study of our current world of global Christianity by Dyron B. Daughrity, titled *To Whom Does Christianity Belong?* The idea is Christianity belongs to everyone who has that relationship through Jesus and a belief in a living, loving God. Daughrity's book showcases many examples of followers of Christ trying to make Christianity their own: African women, Latin American Catholics, American Evangelicals, disciples in the Chinese underground movements, European pastors, Rwandan genocide survivors. "They are all embracing Christianity in their own way according to their own context."[37] This concept of the inclusiveness of the Christian faith

36. Buzzell and Chalquist, *Ecotherapy*, 130.

37. Daughrity, *To Whom Does Christianity Belong?*, 4611.

is also developed by Lemin Sennah in *Whose Religion Is Christianity?* In this work Sennah develops the idea that Christianity in its root form has always been translated into other cultures and contexts since its beginnings. And because of that fact, any culture or context has the ability to do so. Sennah sheds light on this idea, saying, "I have decided to give priority to indigenous response and local appropriation over against missionary transmission and direction, and accordingly have reversed the argument by speaking of the indigenous discovery of Christianity rather than the Christian discovery of indigenous societies."[38] There is thus no intention here to discredit any mystical approach, and instead, in a spirit of inclusion, to acknowledge that those in any given context need to explore their own relationships in a way that relates to that context.

To conclude this review on ecotherapy, I turn to K. Lauren de Boer and her chapter "Healing and the Great Work," which takes us past awakening and empowerment into the inclusive practice of inner peace as a way of achieving self-relation. If we look back over our journey to the spiritual lives of Thurman and Muir, we find they both practiced this search for spiritual inner peace. Thurman, for example, would begin worship services with quiet time to allow others to join him in meditation. De Boer defines the practice in this way:

> Stillness, an inner peace, is the first step in what I call the practice of spiritual ecology. In this sense, I mean spirit as consciousness. To adopt this practice is to apply ecology in a conscious way to our lives, not only through the ecological knowledge that science provides, but through respectful presence, through the breath, by being watchful whenever and wherever we are able. To let this quality of stillness feed our inner intention is to look to the Earth for guidance and to find faith in the powers that brought us into being.[39]

38. Sanneh, *Whose Religion Is Christianity?*, 9.

39. Buzzell and Chalquist, *Ecotherapy*, 274.

In further development of the spiritual breathing practice, de Boer shares a story about the wisdom of inner peace derived from the Dalai Lama:

> As editor of *EarthLight Magazine*, I once interviewed James Thornton, a highly successful litigator for the Natural Resources Defense Council (NRDC). In spite of his stellar success (James had won over one hundred federal cases in defense of the planet), he began to lose heart for the work. He left the NRDC and went on a spiritual quest that led him, eventually, to the Dalai Lama. By the time of his interview, James had a clear question for him: "How do I bring my spiritual practice together with environmental practice?" The Dalai Lama's response was, "You must become confident and positive. Long-term solutions can never come out of an angry mind. You must get over your own anger. Achieve a confident and positive mind. Then help others reach that place." James realized how much of his work had been based on anger. After six months of intense practice, he returned to the United States and founded an organization that teaches wisdom practices to policy makers, social activists, and future leaders.[40]

We might be reminded here about the simplicity of the practice of decluttering our minds and focusing in on our spirit or breath and allowing nature to teach us that practice. We might also be reminded as Christians to have a relationship with Jesus, God, and nature in that simplicity, by seeking Jesus, who describes himself as "Spirit and Life." It is a matter of how we choose to live.

OTHER ACADEMIC RESEARCH ON THE BENEFITS OF SPENDING TIME IN NATURE

While *Forest Bathing* certainly provides a good scientific base for the benefits of the ecological relationship, and while *Ecotherapy* offers much wisdom on the practice of the relationship with nature,

40. Buzzell and Chalquist, *Ecotherapy*, 276.

there has also been significant exploration around this topic in various other academic fields. Although this research remains relatively secular, our higher education systems are increasingly seeing a need to find answers to the broken relationship with nature and respond to the scientific understanding of our environmental crisis. This development might remind us of Wilson's call for cooperation between the humanities and the physical sciences.

The University of Minnesota has a Nature-Based Therapeutics program (NBT) led by Dr. Jean Larson. In a webinar called "An Intro to Nature-Based Therapeutics," Larson gives the program's tagline: "A connection to nature is essential to human health and wellbeing."[41] The program outlines biophilia and suggests the healing power of nature comes from two factors, "access to nature and engagement with nature."[42] What is interesting about this program is that it states in direct terms in what ways the human/nature relationship is beneficial. The first of these comes under the heading of "Attention Restoration Theory," and holds nature provides cognitive benefits by letting the brain rest and replenish. The second is "Stress Reduction Theory" which argues that nature relaxes our parasympathetic nervous system with natural stimuli.

In the endeavor to encourage an ecological spiritual practice, Larson introduces the idea that these two theories of Attention Restoration and Stress Reduction give us the natural ability to attain mindfulness, or the practice of being in the moment in nature. The ideas I have been forwarding in this work, from the spiritual practices of Thurman and Muir to those of the collected work, *Ecotherapy*, revolve around the idea of nature having the ability to guide us towards inner spiritual peace. We now encounter theories that demonstrate how nature helps Christians with this spiritual practice.

This growing attention to the benefits of spending time in nature can be found at other universities also, such as the University of Derby, which has a Nature Connectedness Research Group dedicated to the topic. Other searches of the internet reveal Harvard,

41. Earl E. Bakken Center for Spirituality & Healing, "Nature Heals," 07:35.

42. Earl E. Bakken Center for Spirituality & Healing, "Nature Heals," 09:30.

the University of California, Utah State, McMaster, Cornell, Yale, Penn State, University of Michigan, and Stanford all have online articles about the benefits of spending time in nature. It is safe to say this field of study is here to stay and growing.

CONCLUSION

This review of the benefits of spending time in nature has moved the idea of Christian spiritual ecology into a matter-of-fact reality. It has transcended the theological dualism of the "Great Myth" and the "big lie" to say, yes, it is in our best interest to experience Jesus as spirit and life through a healing relationship with nature.

I have taken up John Cobb's call to write about a new way of living focused on oneness and inclusivity and thus reach a new Christian spiritual ecology. I have provided scientific proof that this ecological relationship is something that should be practiced by Christians. The need to characterize it as a practice and a relationship means Christians can finally move away from a theology that has always struggled to define ecology. By suggesting that we need to pray in order to find the mystery of God in creation, our Christian theologies on the human/nature ecological relationship have hovered around treating the idea as a suggestion or a theory. Always in the background to this approach is the Aristotelian concept of the higher human, or the doctrine of original sin and a tainted humanity in relation to nature. As a result, the idea gets posed in thought rather than as a practice. I have discovered from my research and from discussion with other Christians when describing my own passion for and relationship with nature that I am often referred to Sallie McFague's *Models of God* for a Christian understanding of the ecological relationship. McFague does offer some beautiful descriptions and imagery of the world as the body of God, yet she stops short by saying this is only a metaphor: "Hence, to imagine the world as God's body is to do precisely that: to imagine it that way. It is not to say that the world is God's body or that God is present to us in the world. Those things we do not know; all that resurrection faith can do is imagine the most significant ways to speak of God's presence in one's own time."[43]

This is the very reason for this research on the benefits for Christians of spending time in nature, for it moves us past discussion, theory, or contemplation to say not only is the relationship acceptable, it is beneficial as well. It also honors the inclusivity of nature and does not say we as Christians are the only ones who need to practice this ecological relationship, as it is beneficial for other religions and for the nonreligious as well.

In a sense the journey is complete, having successfully moved from theory to the practice of the ecological relationship. It is now possible to begin with confidence to ask what this might look like as a model of ministry in our churches, and how this model might offer healing in our current world.

43. McFague, *Models Of God*, 844.

Chapter 4: Why The Separation?

> You are already clean because of the word I have spoken to you. Remain in me, as I also remain in you. No branch can bear fruit by itself; it must remain in the vine. Neither can you bear fruit unless you remain in me. I am the vine; you are the branches. If you remain in me and I in you, you will bear much fruit; apart from me you can do nothing. (John 15:3–5)

Before we venture into what CSE has to offer as a practice, we should first address the question: Why do we not already practice it? How have we become so separated and isolated from the natural world that the indoor generation spends 90 percent of their lives indoors not doing so?

"The Nature of Americans" report offers five reasons why this has happened. I will toss in the cosmological perspective from Aristotle of the great chain of being, which is still a dominant understanding of our society, along with Christian doctrines, such as that of original sin, which offers its own cosmology of separation. One finds from looking at these reasons for the separation between the human and nature that such a separation is basically an assumption that humanity has adopted, and this subconsciously. It is not as if we wake in the morning and say to ourselves "I want nothing to do with the natural world." It is simply the way we have developed as humanity, although perhaps with our environmental crisis we are beginning to ponder why our current state is lacking in awareness of the natural world.

"The Nature of Americans" report is from a study conducted by Dr. Stephen Kellert and D. J. Case & Associates between 2015 and 2016. The study offers five reasons for the human/nature separation which are as follows: (1) The places where people live, work, and go to school generally discourage contact with the natural world. (2) Competing priorities for time, attention, and money prevent contact with nature becoming routine. (3) Declining direct dependence on the natural world for livelihoods and substance allows Americans to orient their lives towards other things. (4) New technologies, especially electronic media, distract and captivate. (5) Finally, shifting expectations about what "good" contact to nature ought to be means adults are generally satisfied with the relatively little time they spend outdoors in nature.[1]

One can discern from this study that these reasons for the separation basically point to a shift in human cultural expectations and values. When studying sociology, we find a culture will operate in manner that accords with what it values. Through the general advancement of our technologies, along with our separation cosmologies, we have increasingly created a separation of humanity from nature. Why awareness of this is so important is because it all tends to operate at the level of the subconscious. It is not as if people wake in the morning saying they need to make sure they do not go outside today. Instead, the reasons and time for humans to practice this relationship has slowly vanished from our culture. As we move into the spiritual practice of this ecology, this awareness aspect will be part of the practice itself. We need to begin to cultivate the value of time in our daily lives because contemporary culture will afford neither the time nor the value to doing so.

The *Scala Naturae* concept of Aristotle places creation on a laddered hierarchy of intelligence. Humans are considered more intelligent than other parts of nature and are thus placed higher on the ladder. From a Christian perception, this concept is very similar to the idea of humans having dominion over God's creation as

1. US Fish and Wildlife Service, "New Study."

stated in Genesis and in Ps 8. However, when studying the Trinity, if God's creation is part of that Trinity along with Jesus and the Holy Spirit, it does not make sense to say humanity has the ability to rule or have dominion over God. In reality, a healthy perspective of our authority or dominion depends on the values we are governed by. Dominion over nature does not have to mean that humanity is greater than God and the natural world in the sense of the great chain of being. The concept of dominion is better understood as humanity realizing the miracle of God's creation and seeking to care for it.

As we learn from the Christian spiritualists, the concept of self-realization and becoming one with God supports a Trinitarian concept in which God, Jesus, and the Holy Spirit are three parts of the same entity. The concept of the *Scala Naturae* creates a separation in the Trinity, with humans paradoxically having dominance over nature/God, treating nature as a resource, and valuing it only as a material benefit. As we learn from Irenaeus and the concept of Jesus as the Author of Life, the recapitulating aspect of his teachings offers a different perspective on the concept of dominion. If we are to love God with all our hearts, and if God is within natural creation itself as part of the Trinity, our dominion takes the form of valuing the natural world in the sense of reverence towards God. This then creates a concept of relationship rather than one of separation.

Unfortunately, the separation narrative I discovered during my research reflects the idea that the essence of the natural world is truly different from the essence of the human. There is a prevailing belief that humanity is one thing and the natural world another. This separation is what predominates in our culture. As an ecologist, I think to myself, "Wait a minute, did you not eat food today, drink water, enjoy the sunlight lighting your way?" However, in contemporary human consciousness, it is as if nature is not really an important part of our lives. We can almost do without it. Regardless of the philosophy or faith, this separation narrative has established itself with humanity treated as apart from nature in the way we live our lives. However, the scientific understanding and research on the benefits of spending time in nature reveal this to be in contradiction with the truth.

The truth is that we do have a need to relate to nature. Whether or not we choose to relate is an individual choice. The changed approach which we are calling Christian spiritual ecology celebrates a life that is in relationship with nature, God, and Jesus. To help envision what this nonseparated ecology lifestyle looks like as we move away from the separation narrative, it is time to explore the ecology of human/nature togetherness.

Chapter 5: The Human/Nature Ecology of Togetherness

> Before long, the world will not see me anymore, but you will see me. Because I live, you also will live. On that day you will realize that I am in my Father, and you are in me, and I am in you. (John 14:19–20)

Ecological anthropology is the study of how the human ecosystem relates to nature's ecosystem. The topics studied in this field range from early hunter-gathering societies that lived in a sustainable relationship with natural ecosystems to current research from NASA that the relationships between the human ecosystem and the ecosystems of nature have become the greatest contributing factor to the environmental crisis.

In simple terms, through time our human way of life has become increasingly isolated from the ecosystem needs of the natural world. This isolation is manifest in the 90 percent of our time we spend indoors. Basically, having become increasingly separate from the ecosystem of the natural world, we are at the point of considering human beings as having no need for an ecological relationship with nature. We have arrived at the belief, and this includes Christians, that we can live apart from the natural ecosystem, and indeed, that human existence is actually better off this way. We have basically succeeded in putting the theory of the great chain of being into practice. Yet, as we have seen here in this research, the truth from the sciences is that both humanity and the natural world are negatively impacted by this separation.

I would like to suggest that maybe there is some common sense and reality at play here in our definition of the human/nature ecological relationship. I have found it interesting in conversations with church and nonchurch folks about my work on this topic that the responses are often, "I have always believed that being in nature is being with God," or "I see the presence of God in the natural world." This sounds a lot like common sense, or an understanding that this is how things are.

For in reality we can all admit we need clean air to breathe, water to cleanse ourselves, and good food for nourishment. To think we can realistically live a life separated from the natural world does not make sense. It's physically not possible. Yet we live in a separation narrative and live indoors as if nature were just something "out there."

A human theory is just that, a theory derived from the opinion of a human being. I am admittedly doing that right now. Yet if we view the natural world and ecosystem (which as Christians we would call God's creation) objectively, without imposing human thought, and ponder what a tree believes and so forth, we will discover nature does quite well on its own without human theory and becomes very life-giving. Such an approach is a bit like Von Humboldt's ecology or perhaps like Muir's understanding of the inventions of God.

We can find this approach in surfing culture: i.e., the idea that we humans have overthought our existence to the point of separating ourselves from creation. During my studies in seminary, I had difficulty with certain theologies that suggested a separation between God and the natural world, or an understanding that Jesus is only in heaven and not fully incarnate in resurrected form, as in the Gospels. I had trouble with theologies portraying a fearsome God compared to the loving God of compassion Jesus teaches about in the Gospels. I was perplexed by the urge to hold on to these human theories and theologies even though they really did not make sense anymore.

I believe it is important to be able to abandon human theories, as they simply represent someone's opinion at some point in time. Humans once theorized the earth was flat. Do we still believe that? The idea that humanity is separate from the natural world has been supported by Christian theologies and human theories. Does it still really make sense? Or have we perhaps overthought our existence?

In the study of ecological anthropology, we obviously cannot go back to living like primitive cultures. However, in the sense of an ecological relationship, we can begin to value the relationship with nature afresh for the betterment of humanity and the natural world.

We can move the definition of the human/nature relationship from one of separation towards one of togetherness. In urging for care and compassion for God and others, there is a togetherness teaching of grace and compassion from Jesus, which we will look into more deeply in the forthcoming discussions about practice. Christians are comfortable with the concept of being stewards of the natural world, which is fine. Yet for the practice of togetherness, a more holistic approach is required. We need to realize that God and creation are also stewards; they are our stewards. This realization can help us avoid the separation narrative that suggests we humans are a little smarter "over here," and so we need to take care of nature "over there."

The reason for this argument for togetherness is because a great spiritual loss occurs in separation. The idea being supported here is that we literally only become aware of how God created our souls through a relationship with nature. We find our own unique spirituality in that relationship. We can then say Christian spiritual ecology is about relating with nature and finding God, Jesus, and ourselves.

Chapter 6: Togetherness

> Forget the former things;
>   do not dwell on the past.
> See, I am doing a new thing!
>   Now it springs up; do you not perceive it?
> I am making a way in the wilderness
>   and streams in the wasteland.
> (Isaiah 43:18–19)

INTRODUCTION

To recapitulate the journey thus far: First, we have transcended the theological debate to take Christian spiritual ecology into the present age to finally align faith with the sciences. This is something E. O. Wilson and John Cobb called for. Because this is a new approach, the task places us in what John Cobb called a new way of living and a new perspective. The approach breaks free of past dualistic Christian thinking to embrace the ecological concept of oneness and self-realization inspired by Gandhi. The alignment of belief with science enables us to confidently say that as Christians we should practice and encourage the human/nature ecological relationship.

We have now encountered territory in Christianity of the sort that ancient Celtic Christianity once encouraged. We are now empowered by scientific research to suggest how we might heal these relationships: the human side, the nature side, and the ecological relationship itself. Looking at the healing of these three aspects of Christian ecology is the task of this chapter. In the simplicity of breath, spirit, and teaching from this new field for Christians, let us take a lesson from the meditative teaching of nature and not go backwards by overthinking this. The concept I have been developing to articulate the human/nature relationship is one of awareness and practice. It is a focus on breath and how we live our lives in interaction. Often this is something we as human beings take for granted. Yet we are reminded by Saint Francis' sermonette to the birds of the need to remain grateful. We might be surprised to discover that much of humanity is indeed looking for healing and would wish to be grateful to God and creation. We just need to create the space and encourage the teaching for this to happen.

This leads to my reason for describing this work as a journey, because we now are in uncharted waters of the healing of humanity and nature, and the relationship between them. As Christians we are now encouraging the relationship. Unlike our dualistic past, we are creating a new space for Christians to explore. It is exciting. It is like the feeling of entering a garden in spring and seeing what is being brought back to life, or of venturing into the mountains to heights that align us with the clouds.

HEALING THE HUMAN/NATURE RELATIONSHIP

The interconnectedness that Cobb wrote about has suffered, and continues to suffer, neglect. This may be one way to describe the human/nature ecological relationship. In light of the research into the indoor generation, with its 90 percent of indoor time, we become aware that we are typically only tending to this relationship 10 percent of the time, and it can even be asked how much of this 10 percent is actually focused on the relationship. As a society we basically do not value the relationship with the natural world.

Personally, I often think of time spent in nature as similar to receiving communion. If we think about how intentional Jesus was in describing his own resurrection in earthly elements through which we are spiritually nourished, he makes it simple. "I am the bread of life." There is no long coded creed we must memorize and recite.

Communion is important because when we receive it, in our thanksgiving prayers we acknowledge being spiritually nourished at the table. Something happens in our earthly element in the process of eating the bread. Something from nature and the earth has the power to enrich the spirit. (Here we might recall the science-backed concept of biophilia.)

Perhaps if I had proposed this idea to the reader a hundred years ago—i.e., that spending time in nature is like communion, through which we experience a spiritual enrichment—I would have faced opposition. Prove it, someone might have said. But in our time we have the proof. There is scientific evidence to support the argument that we are better off when we spend more time in nature. The nourishment or communion is real. And thus the healing of the relationship comes from encouraging the relationship. But practically speaking, how might we increase the average amount of time people spend out of doors?

Possible ways of spending time in nature as a practice will be explored in the conclusion to this work. The focus here is simply on how we as Christians might promote this insight in our church communities. We need to advocate for interconnectedness. In the neglected ecological relationship, there is an obvious balance or harmony issue. There is no interaction purely for the sake of the other. To achieve balance and harmony, one party needs to seek out the other in order to understand its needs and then act in support of these. The other side does the same in return. To take an example from relationship counseling: we are aware of the need for balance between the two parties and teach about it. A healthy human relationship requires communication, mutual understanding, and support of each other's needs.

It is the same with music. In music different notes fit together in different patterns to produce sounds pleasing to the ear, a sense of harmony. There is an interconnectedness between the notes of the melody and the rhythms of the sound. Music in which one part does something independently of the other without interaction or exchange would not make sense. Whatever the musical style, the parts of the piece work together to support one another. This is what interconnection in a relationship is about. Some might even say that supporting one another is the meaning of life. This lesson of balance and harmony in the form of relationship and interconnectedness is also repeatedly manifest in nature, for example, through photosynthesis and the harmonious workings of water, plants, and sunlight.

If as Christians we turn towards Jesus and this teaching, we find he is all about healing relationships. To forgive, to "love one another as I have loved you," and to love God with all our heart is Jesus' teaching of togetherness.

Our self-realizers, Thurman and Muir, give us the language to talk about God and nature in one breath. They are the same thing. Muir speaks of the "inventions of God" and Thurman of a place where he was rooted in life, in nature, and existence. As Christian ecologists, we can then say that to love God with all our heart is to love nature with all our heart. Terms such "Jesus as the Author of Life" and his description of a living God are referring to human beings and nature. Baptism is a good example here, for the living God can and does heal through the waters.

Earlier in my academic journey I was thinking of calling this book *On Earth as in Heaven*. The Lord's Prayer is all about finding relational harmony and balance. To realize heaven on earth is to realize God within creation with all our heart. The awareness I am promoting here is that "God's will be done in nature as in heaven." I have realized as a pastor this prayer is appropriate in every situation, because it expresses the realization of God's presence here with us on earth. That is to say, God is with us. God is within nature. It is a call for the realization of balance, harmony, oneness, and interconnection, and it is also a call for us to be grateful and forgiving, that we might help nurture that balance of oneness.

In the research into the benefits of spending time in nature, we moved from the biophilia hypothesis, which is much like Gandhi's deep ecology concept of oneness, to tangible research that demonstrates this thinking is true. We do benefit mentally and physically from the relationship with nature. However, to turn towards relating with God in nature is a whole other project, and even though it is something that is supported by the research, we are not doing so, and with tragic results.

Therefore, the practice of a Christian spiritual ecology is encouraged here. So how exactly do we live out the relationship with nature in practice? This is something I believe we need to become comfortable with. It does not mean we all have to live on organic farms and raise our own food and in that way spend the majority of our time in nature. It is more about simply saying in our daily living, "How might we heal the way we as humans relate with nature?" and taking simple steps with a view to our own health and for the sake of the health of nature. We already know there are benefits in that. So now we are encouraged in terms of healing and reconciliation to see how we can improve the balance of the relationship.

As mentioned, there are many ways of doing this. As I write, I can hear a pileated woodpecker calling out. There is one right here, and I am listening to this endangered voice of nature at the same time as we are learning the quietness of nature is becoming endangered. As individuals, each of our ways of relating to nature will be different, as noted previously with reference to the inclusivity of the relationship. I believe the only unified call to emerge from research into the ecological relationship is simply that something needs to change in that relationship. If the relationship is currently problematic, both for humanity and the natural world, how might we change it?

We are familiar with research into the environmental crisis and ways we could be living differently to better attend to the needs of the earth, because the problem has become common knowledge. However, in terms of the beneficial aspect of this present research, what I am now suggesting is that there is meaning and wellbeing to be found in the relationship. It is not just the right thing to do. We are lost as a culture because of our disconnection from nature, and thus we value AI technology over the information we gather from a walk in a forest. Yet when we study sociology, we realize that what society values governs how it will operate. This is much like the concept in process theology that says how we relate with one another and God will dictate the future.

If we as Christians can learn how to value the ecological relationship and teach this as a model of ministry, passing on what has already been learned from scientific research, the results will be beneficial. We are then looking at the deeper reasons behind all of the world's current problems with the environment and with human physical and mental health. John Muir's baptism in the mountains led to the preservation of our national parks. His valuing of God's inventions led to the healing and preservation of nature. The same can be said of Thurman's understanding of the natural teaching of dignity for all, for this led to the civil rights movement. So then, I am advocating the importance of valuing the human/nature relationship as a model of ministry, since we know doing so can have profound effects.

We might think of valuing the human/nature relationship in terms of the concept of self-realization discussed earlier. In relating to nature as Christians, we can find deeper meaning in the reading of the Scriptures, and a deeper meaning of the place of our churches in the community. We might then imagine the church as a central location in the community for teaching the value of the ecological relationship.

The common thread joining all the various individuals discussed thus far is that they all deeply appreciated the ecological human/nature relationship. Psalm 65 (NIV) reads,

> 1 Praise awaits you, our God, in Zion;
> to you our vows will be fulfilled.
> 2 You who answer prayer,
> to you all people will come.
> 3 When we were overwhelmed by sins,
> you forgave our transgressions.
> 4 Blessed are those you choose
> and bring near to live in your courts!
> We are filled with the good things of your house,
> of your holy temple.

5 You answer us with awesome and righteous deeds,
God our Savior,
the hope of all the ends of the earth
and of the farthest seas,
6 who formed the mountains by your power,
having armed yourself with strength,
7 who stilled the roaring of the seas,
the roaring of their waves,
and the turmoil of the nations.
8 The whole earth is filled with awe at your wonders;
where morning dawns, where evening fades,
you call forth songs of joy.

9 You care for the land and water it;
you enrich it abundantly.
The streams of God are filled with water
to provide the people with grain,
for so you have ordained it.
10 You drench its furrows and level its ridges;
you soften it with showers and bless its crops.
11 You crown the year with your bounty,
and your carts overflow with abundance.
12 The grasslands of the wilderness overflow;
the hills are clothed with gladness.
13 The meadows are covered with flocks
and the valleys are mantled with grain;
they shout for joy and sing.

This is very similar to Saint Francis' "Canticle of Creatures" and John Muir's spiritual writings. We might also think of songs such as "For the Beauty of the Earth" or "God's Eye Is on the Sparrow" for an evocation of awareness of God within creation. Then there is the language from Thurman and from Celtic Christianity of Jesus as the "Author of Life," and as being within the natural creation. It is in the appreciation of this understanding that self-realization happens. Not only do we as a Christian church have the resources and language to advocate for ecological practice, we can also back belief in the practice with scientific evidence of the mental and physical health benefits. This model of ministry thus moves us past just speaking about environmental justice into what

Cobb is attributed in writing about a new way of life, or into something like what Irenaeus is attributed with saying when he spoke of Christ "recapitulating" creation.

To talk about appreciating God's creation as Christians in a relationship with nature, and understanding Jesus as the "Author of Life," sounds simple. However, there is a need to go further than this and to say not only do we appreciate God's creation in a relationship with nature and Jesus as the "Author of Life," but we proclaim it also. If we as a church were to spread information out there on the benefits of the ecological relationship, imagine the positive impact. Is this not what Jesus has called us to do? "To love one another as I have loved you." Is not helping someone discover a better mental and physical way of being a way of showing them love? Is not living in a healing relationship with nature a way of loving God with all our hearts?

When I have shared the statistics about our indoor generation, people have been shocked by the figures. Part of what is going on here in this unawareness is the assumption that there is nothing inherently wrong with how we have arrived here, or with the development of technology and science that has created the conditions that enable us to spend 90 percent of our time inside. Technology and science will continue to develop and there is nothing inherently wrong with that. However, there is a great need to keep in balance our attention to the sciences and our studies of the humanities. As O. E. Wilson noted about the need for awareness of the ecological relationship, "separated completely from the natural world we will find little ultimate meaning from the remainder of life."[1] It is the intention of this work to align the sciences and humanities, and to accept that we live in a secular world that trusts the sciences. Now the sciences are advocating the benefits of spending time in nature, and the churches could do so also. This model of ministry can help our world realize how it is missing out on this important ecological relationship.

To conclude this section on healing the human/nature relationship, I offer a reflection on the practical benefit of my own

1. Wilson. *Biophilia*, 82.

field research into pollinator awareness. This is in response to the reader's hypothetical question: "How do we teach the value of this ecological relationship in our churches?"

We are entering the fall of the third year of having pollinator gardens at my church, and this third summer they really flourished. We had good rainfall this summer as I did not have to water except perhaps a couple of times and the root systems have grown strong, sending up a lot of new plants and filling in the space. There are three gardens on the church property. I designed them to be large, one in the front of the church, another to the north side of the church, and a large one on the south side with a path going through it and a bench to sit on along the path.

Our church is the first thing you see when you drive into our small historic community. The neo-Gothic historic building greets you as you drive in under a bridge. And so the three pollinator gardens are on full display, along with my many hours spending time tending to them. Neighbors joke about me being the gardener instead of the pastor of the church. Many of the plants we began the gardens with three years ago were rescued from original pollinator gardens at the original campus of a nearby seminary. So, there is really a powerful resurrection aspect to that part of the story alone. These plants that were originally given by donors to the seminary out of concern for the environment have found new life and live on at our church in Northland.

There are plants in the gardens given by church members who are no longer living and these continue to grow and spread as we are reminded of those loved ones' presence in heaven. We have many plants given to us as donations by community neighbors who do not belong to the church and their plants flourish also. Community gardeners in the fall collect seeds from the gardens for winter sowing and a continued propagation and sharing of these plants. So, they are true community gardens as people often walk their dogs there, giving appreciation for the sight and color of the flowers. In the summer there are butterflies, dragonflies, and a variety of bees, some endangered, out dancing around the flowers. Community members, both of the congregation and beyond, see these gardens and the value we accord them as a church by having them on our property. Appreciation has been voiced many times and we have thus succeeded in teaching their value.

We are poised at a very particular time in history. The environmental crisis, the mental health crisis, the increased level of risk of disease from not enough physical activity, research on the indoor generation, and the effects of too much screen time all have in common separation in the human/nature ecological relationship.[2] The relationship is literally crying in agony from both the human and the nature perspectives, which we will look at next. And while it is wonderful at the level of university education to see the beginning of a trend that will hopefully keep going in addressing this broken relationship, there is also a need at the community level to bring about awareness of this lost value of the relationship. We as Christian churches in ministry have the opportunity to seize this moment and find our deeper identity and teach about tending to this relationship as a way of ministry. This is not so we can be great, but so human beings can realize the greatness of God's creation, that the natural world might be celebrated, as in Ps 65 and in the hymn "How Great Thou Art." And so, through the natural teaching of inclusiveness we can reach out to our brothers and sisters in this increasingly global multifaith world with this common interest.

HEALING NATURE

From my own research on the environment over the last few years, I am aware we have moved in consideration of global warming from theories about how it could be happening to now having the science behind the theories and for the most part a societal acceptance that it is real. What the sciences are also revealing is that the way we as humans relate to the natural world is the main contributing factor to global warming. Hence this quote from NASA: "Since systematic scientific assessments began in the 1970s, the

2. Psychiatry.org, "American Adults Express." Minnesota Department of Health, "TV, Screen Time, and Health."

influence of human activity on the warming of the climate system has evolved from theory to established fact."3 The imbalance in this harmful way we as humans are relating to nature stems from the fact we basically give our own needs priority over those of nature.

Do we wake in the morning as if in a relationship and say, "Nature/God, what are you in need of today?" We are so out of balance even proposing the question sounds odd. However, that is the state of existence we need to get to quickly if we are to save and heal the natural world. Here again there is need for the Christian church to take this ecological relationship as a model of ministry. Belief systems, such as the value systems I discussed in the previous section on healing the relationship, have an effect on how we live our lives. If we as churches accept the undertaking to make changes in lifestyle that take into consideration global warming and the need of the environment, the impact could be wonderful in terms of the global Christian church. If we as Christians were now to become ecologists and practice the lifestyle, imagine the difference.

If we think of the indoor generation and time spent inside, part of the problem is that the relationship with nature does not seem real. For the most part in our artificial human world, we do not need to take nature into consideration as a farmer might. We do not need to do so in order to get by. That is part of the problem. And if we do not teach it from our churches, where is the awareness going to develop? There literally is a need right now for the message that we should be considering our lifestyle in relationship to others, and to God/nature. How else will this message and teaching get out into the community if not from religious institutions?

This is an issue of passion. Teaching about the physical and mental benefits of nature for humanity will create passion for healing the natural world. Surfing culture is known by its character to be very environmentally friendly as a result of the passion and wellbeing its members receive from spending a lot of time outside. There is in turn a concern for the natural world. The same could

3. NASA Science, "Causes of Climate Change."

happen with our churches. I witnessed it in my teaching classes on pollinators where people went from not knowing how to identify common milkweeds to planting them in their yards.

In considering nature, there is also a wisdom we as a culture are missing out on. There is an essential goodness in nature implied in this research. The benefits of the human/nature ecological relationship I am suggesting stem from the fact that nature itself has an intrinsic knowledge of what is good for our bodies and minds. Our own human intelligence is better off infused with the wisdom of nature. It has been my intention in writing this book to align belief with science. It is known in the world of science that Orthodox Judaism has long embraced this relationship between faith and science. Rabbi Joel Padowitz writes about this relationship as follows: "By delving into even the basics of physics, chemistry, and biology we can begin to truly gain a glimpse of God's genius—more importantly—foster a conscious awareness of His loving, active presence in our lives."[4]

If one is a Christian and believes in a creator God, the study of nature through the sciences is a lens into the incredible "Inventions of God," as Muir put it.[5] And whether or not one is a believer, from the standpoint of artistic appreciation, the intricate workings of nature are amazing. Influenced by the notion of a great chain of being, as humans we unfortunately get caught up in our own intelligence to the point where we think AI is some otherworldly invention of intelligence, yet it cannot produce a dragonfly or spider. In the way it lives, nature is extremely intelligent. Take for example photosynthesis, the process where plants take sunlight, carbon dioxide, and water and turn them into oxygen and sugar. That is amazing. Then there is the way our water cycles work in evaporation, clouds, seas, rivers, and lakes, all communicating and once again amazing. We have led ourselves into becoming an indoor generation that has a fridge full of food, internet, and all kinds of entertainment through the television. We think little of nature. However, it is from nature that all the materials for our

4. Aish.com, "Sacred Science."

5. Stoll, "God and John Muir."

homes, technology, and food come. Yet we are unaware how nature sustains us and is in us, as in the self-realization understanding. We are responding to the environmental crisis at an alarmingly slow rate. What if our dogs or family members were to develop a temperature and grow sick, as is the case with global warming? We would rush out and spend all kinds of money and do whatever possible to heal them. Yet the intelligence of nature and how it gives us everything we need for life is suffering intensely right now and we are basically indifferent.

Psychologists call it the ego. Christianity calls it sin (in the Hebrew understanding of missing the mark or failed relationship with God). It is a place where a person is self-absorbed or caught up in themselves. There are studies in religion and psychology about how we might free ourselves of this energy. On a large scale, and derived from thoughts such as the great chain of being, this is where we—humanity as a whole—are at. As a culture we are so human-consumed that we spend 90 percent of our time inside. This is behind the idea I have been developing in this work: i.e., the self-realization or spiritual freedom from ego that occurs in nature experiences. Nature has the ability to help us get over ourselves, yet we currently are so self-absorbed we have cut nature out of our lives. Once again, the need is for our churches to take the lead in this discussion. We need the ability not to take ourselves so seriously. Having this ability gives us the opportunity to look at and appreciate the intelligence of nature. Take for example the inventions of humanity when we are able to get over ourselves and look to nature for inspiration. Velcro was inspired by burrs; much aviation was inspired by different types of birds and how they fly; wetsuits by shark skins; buildings and art by the way spiders construct their habitats; solar panels were inspired by photosynthesis; humpback fins inspired wind turbines: animal limbs inspired earthquake resistant bridges; the feet of geckos inspired nontoxic adhesives. The list goes on and on.

As with the previous topic of healing the ecological relationship, we find that in realizing the value of nature we are enabled to see its preciousness. This is an idea that can be developed in the next section on healing humanity. How do we get this generation to peel away its indoor layer and realize the preciousness of nature? Realizing the intelligence of nature is of value is the result of looking at ways of healing nature. Rather than overthinking this, what is required is appreciation of the intelligence of nature as a way of understanding the healing of the ecological relationship. In this current era we have not fully encountered the possibilities that can emerge from aligning our sciences with our faith. In this journey we are on the verge of emerging anew as a Christian church and describing to this isolated generation that not only are we missing out on the benefits of appreciating nature, but also the benefits we could gain from learning from its intelligence, because we are a generation that has decided to remove itself from God/nature.

HEALING HUMANITY

I have already covered this topic in the previous discussion on the human benefits of spending time in nature. This then created the opportunity to look into healing the nature/human relationship and to look at healing nature itself by realizing its intelligence and the intelligence of a creator God. However, to get to the point of healing these ecological relationships, we need to awaken the self-absorbed human collective mind to say, yes, we can benefit from this. We are missing out!

This is the task before us in this model of ministry. We can describe the benefits for nature and humanity in healing this relationship all day long. However, if our current generation cannot find the ability to peel away its indoor self, there is little hope. In my own life I think of my personal ecological awareness as a gift. It was given to me by my mother at a young age. Looking back, I was a very depressed and moody child and my mother would encourage me to "go outside and get some fresh air and you will feel better." In those formative years we lived by a small lake with a grove of woods nearby. I explored and engaged with nature with my Dalmatian dog by my side. In the evenings I would sit by the waters, watch the sunset, and talk to God.

That connection or gift has never gone away and has been the predominant theme in my life from the redwoods forests to the Rocky Mountains, and to large river valleys. I have intentionally lived my life in areas where I was enthralled by the natural beauty around me. The interaction with Jesus entered my life when I returned home after these travels and went to church and allowed the music, Scripture, and messages to heal me as I learned about forgiveness and how much Jesus loved me and others. I went into seminary with these convictions about the healing aspect of nature and the healing aspect of the Gospels. My mentor, who had confirmed me from my home church, was at that time suffering from early-onset dementia. There is a whole other side story in my spiritual journey with him. As the reader knows, it is a horrible disease with no answers. After visits I would find myself immersed in the pollinator gardens with dragonflies landing on my shoulders, soaking in the sun, and the smell of the plants. In the evening I could feel their light comforting me. This was the same gift given to me by my mother.

As Christians we have honestly struggled to find language that can embrace this ecological relationship. Yes, we have theorized about creation being filled with the presence of God, yet saying we should worship God in nature has been difficult for us. As a Christian, for me to say I am guided by the spirit of the trees would sound really off. At the same time, as discussed in this work, we have come to see ourselves as beyond and more intelligent than nature, leading to further separation. To this we can add our development as a society to the point where we have become almost isolated from nature.

Thurman and Muir offer us a gift here in the concept of self-realization as a way of encouraging people to seek time in nature. In this research I am able to further identify this concept and idea as biophilia, a vast self, oneness, interconnectedness, and deep ecology. I am also able to scientifically back up the idea that it is literally beneficial to our physical and mental health to align our faith with our science. This is a value we now have before us that can be presented in our churches for the greater good of the community.

In my first doctoral class on this topic I gave a presentation on setting aside time for relating to nature every day. The response from other students was to ask if I could create a program for them, which for the purposes of this work I call a model of ministry. Then, for this topic on healing humanity, how as a church do we encourage people to get outside more often? It sounds simple, but we all know in our era we live in a fast-paced world where time is very limited, and maybe even a needed resource for a lot of people. We run out of time each day with our extremely busy schedules. We even may think time in our days for the peace of nature is as endangered as the quiet of the natural world itself.

I propose that this lack of time for a relationship with nature is somewhat bound to our material needs. I in no way claim that there is anything wrong with material needs or that we should deny ourselves anything. The problem is that as a culture, we believe we can obtain happiness and joy through our material lives. Here we might consider how commercials sell products. The characters in the commercials are changed because the material products they have acquired have brought happiness. This is not to say that our sciences and material products cannot be very beneficial in our day-to-day living. The idea here is that only having a materialistic viewpoint can limit our ability to realize the need for and value of this nature connection. In *The Book of Joy*, there is an account of a meeting between the Dalai Lama and Archbishop Desmond Tutu in which they highlight our current world and materialistic viewpoint:

> The problem is that our world and our education remain focused exclusively on external, materialistic values. We are not concerned enough with our inner values. Those who grow up with this kind of education live a materialistic life and eventually the whole society becomes materialistic. But this culture is not sufficient to tackle our human problems. The real problem is here," the Dalai Lama said, pointing to his head. The Archbishop tapped his chest with his fingers to emphasize the heart

> as well. "And here," the Dalai Lama echoed. "Mind and heart." Materialistic values cannot give us peace of mind. So we really need to focus on our inner values, our true humanity. Only this way can we have peace of mind—and more peace in our world. A lot of the problems we are facing are our own creation, like war and violence. Unlike a natural disaster, these problems are created by humans ourselves. "I feel there is a big contradiction," the Dalai Lama continued. "There are seven billion human beings and nobody wants to have problems or suffering, but there are many problems and much suffering, most of our own creation. Why?" He was speaking now directly to the Archbishop, who was nodding in agreement. "Something is lacking. As one of the seven billion human beings, I believe everyone has the responsibility to develop a happier world. We need, ultimately, to have a greater concern for others' well-being. In other words, kindness or compassion, which is lacking now. We must pay more attention to our inner values. We must look inside."[6]

Here we have a very elegant description of this material viewpoint along with encouragement of the inward self-realization I am advocating.

I believe the materialistic viewpoint and lack of time are related. I caution myself against prescribing any model of ministry as a way of trying to tell folks how many material goods they should have and how much time they should spend connecting in nature. I have no way of knowing this for each individual, since for each person this will look different. I am nevertheless able to affirm connecting with God in nature is beneficial and so finding time in our lives for this is essential. And so, for a model of ministry, we are able to give voice to the spiritual ecological relationship by talking about the tragedies of the broken relationship and by encouraging people to self-realization. I have brought to light here the fact that time itself is the issue in healing humanity: all that indoor time and the materialistic lives various people have described. It is truly a

6. Dalai Lama and Tutu, *Book of Joy*, 29–30.

question of how people freely spend their time and how they value how that time is spent.

Once one has the time for the ecological connection, the question then turns to what exactly constitutes the self-realization process. I believe Thurman and Muir give us fine examples of what it is about: it is simply taking in nature. Muir describes his baptism in the Sierra Nevadas as taking in his natural surrounding through his senses, in a similar way as forest bathing, and that really was all that was required. It is the same for Thurman in his description of taking in the sounds and sights of the ocean, which impressed upon his inner being a place of comfort and peace that he could carry in relationship as encouragement in his life. Our first ecological description from Von Humboldt also entailed a subjective view of the self-awareness of nature.

I might add here that Christians might think of it as taking in Scripture. We all might have a different interpretation of a Bible text from perceiving different aspects through our senses. Yet in the same way Scripture and the Gospels can spiritually guide us, the same can be said for self-realization in nature. We have just never allowed ourselves to say that as Christians. What might the future look like from this new Christian perspective?

Chapter 7: Moving Forward

DOES CHRISTIAN SPIRITUAL ECOLOGY MAKE SENSE?

> "You are the salt of the earth. But if the salt loses its saltiness, how can it be made salty again? It is no longer good for anything, except to be thrown out and trampled underfoot.
>
> "You are the light of the world. A town built on a hill cannot be hidden. Neither do people light a lamp and put it under a bowl. Instead they put it on its stand, and it gives light to everyone in the house. In the same way, let your light shine before others, that they may see your good deeds and glorify your Father in heaven." (Matthew 5:13–16)

As described by one of my seminary professors, the point of writing a book is to find that empty spot on your bookshelf where your topic will fit in and contribute to the overall library. We began with the definition of Christian spiritual ecology as something that moves us from theory to actual practice. This then brings us to the definition of Christian spiritual ecology as an awareness that by developing our ecological/relationship with the natural world we are then living out a spiritual/life with God and Jesus.

The problem lies in the Christian theology of the past, with its doctrine of original sin functioning as a "Great Myth" or "big lie" about the relationship with nature, with Aristotle's great chain of being, and with our own metaphorical speech about God and

Jesus in the natural world, which avoids language that talks of the worship of God in the natural world through a relationship with Jesus as Author of Life. This issue is resolved for us as Christians by finally understanding that having a right healing relationship with nature is to have a right healing relationship with God and Jesus. And so, in order to fill the gap, this work has focused on the ecological relationship rather than on metaphor and theory.

We supported this idea with the examples of Thurman and Muir, who provide vivid imagery of what this spiritual relationship can look like, and the self-realization of oneness that is experienced in the relationship. Next, we fact-checked the concept of this way of life against current scientific research on the mental and physical health benefits of that relationship and spending time in nature, thereby aligning belief about the ecological relationship with the current sciences, rather than with past theories based on outdated science.

We then looked at what this model of ministry means for the human/nature relationship itself, which is in a state of neglect according to research into the habits of the indoor generation. We also looked at the human aspect, where there are increasing mental health issues in children and adults which came to light through an exploration of forest bathing, ecotherapy, and nature-based therapeutics. And finally, concerns about nature were supported by information from NASA and the UN indicating that the human/nature relationship is the greatest contributing factor to global warming.

To speak plainly, we can say through this research and work that yes, there is absolutely a need for this model of ministry in our current world. While it is good to see research in this ecological relationship growing as a trend within our universities, in our communities, where we take just one day out of the year as "Earth Day," the relationship would benefit from being advocated for weekly in our churches.

So yes, Christian spiritual ecology does make sense. Information on the indoor generation, global warming, and individual human crises supports the ministry need for a message about the healing aspect of the relationship with nature. The church is poised to create a much-needed paradigm shift in our community and global world. As ecumenical churches, we are getting comfortable with concepts like "green church" and "environmental justice programs." This gives rise to a wonderful trend where churches are looking at recycling programs, advocating for environmentally friendly policies, and, if affordable, having their churches run on clean energy and so forth. Yet this model needs to fit into any church wherever they are at. Because this is a model of ministry rather than a programming or business model, the point here is to teach about the benefits of the ecological relationship and encourage Christians to find their own self-realization. This can be done in any church setting.

Aware of my passion for the Christian church and my passion for nature as a surfer, my aunt once sent me an article on Surf Church in Porto, Portugal. I treated the article as if it were a work of art, for it showed the pastor holding out a hand of blessing with surfboards in the background. The article had the title "At This Church Parishioners Surf Before They Worship." I thought that was amazing and I wanted to go and worship with those folks someday. I also imagine that somewhere there is a Christian church that has been able to go totally clean energy and has some kind of amazing green space where their gardens flow into the sanctuary. That would also be wonderful. Yet I realize there are many churches in the middle of urban settings with limited green space. However, they also have the ability and need to practice this ecological relationship in whatever way possible.

To evaluate means to determine the nature, quality, or value of something. The center of this work is the scientific research that supports the thesis that, yes, we do benefit from spending time in nature. This center has been woven from the theory of biophilia, and proof from the practice of forest bathing and the therapeutic benefits of spending time in nature. The field of ecotherapy has described this same center as the "vast self." Then, going back in time, we found the very influential spiritual practice of this same center in the form of "self-realization" in the lives and works of

Thurman and Muir. It has been thus possible through this research to show the value of this center and of the human/nature ecological relationship. This is an evaluation of value; it is the forgotten song from Celtic Christianity, which is tragically lost in our current world.

Fifty years ago John Cobb asked "*Is It Too Late?*" The research is clear that we are not valuing this relationship at tragic cost for humanity and the natural world. To answer Cobb's question and his call for a new lived relationship, we can look to the article from NPR entitled "Americans Spending Less Time In Nature," which reveals outdoor activities such as camping and fishing have been on a downward trend since the 1980s. Time spent in nature decreased 1 percent per year from 25 percent to just 18 percent in 2008.[1] In research from 2017, "The Nature of Americans" national report indicates this time spent outside is continuing to decrease: "It is increasingly normal to spend little time outside."[2] And now we have research indicating the indoor generation spends 90 percent of their time inside.[3] Not only have we not heeded Cobb's call from fifty years ago, we are going further and further in the other direction with this ecological relationship. Jesus tells us in the Gospels not to lose our salt, and to have, in other words, a salty spirit. What salt represented spiritually in his time was a relationship. It was used in the sense of purification in the relationship with God, and was also seen as a symbol of a relationship of friendship (i.e., sharing salt with someone, so as not to lose the relationship). And so we have lost this core of our being, the vast self, our ability to find self-realization. The results of the loss of this ecological relationship and the loss of value spending time in nature mean there is a greater need for ministry in this area than ever before.

1. NPR News, "Americans Spending Less Time in Nature."
2. US Fish and Wildlife Service, "New Study."
3. American Lung Association, "Lung Association Launches."

WHERE DO WE GO FROM HERE?

Writing this book has transformed me. My seminary advisor and professor in my dissertation class both urged me that my topic was too large and that I needed to focus in on something. So, I chose research on the benefits of spending time in nature. In doing so, I originally had no intention of taking the deep ecology of Gandhi, self-realization from Muir and Thurman, and intertwining them with the lost song from Celtic Christianity, which then becomes biophilia and so forth. From my passion for God, Jesus, and nature I simply chose topics and research that spoke to that.

And as I pursued the writing of this work and saw how the construction of the connections all led like strands to support the center, it reminded me of a natural phenomenon such as a snowflake or flower. Thurman described his realization that "nature is a balm for the soul,"[4] and that led to the center. Muir's baptism in the mountains and literal description of his self-realization led to the center. Cobb's call for interconnectedness led to the center. Biophilia and the idea we have a biological need to find self-realization led towards the center. The vast self from ecotherapy then tied the threads to the center, with scientific research on the benefits of the relationship attached to another ground weaving towards the center. This work goes beyond me. It is a credit to these individuals and their passion for the nature relationship and with Jesus as the Author of Life, and it speaks clearly about the need for us as humans to relate with nature.

I believe the answer to the question "Where do we go from here?" is that there is need for the message to get out about the relationship. When I shared with my church that the indoor generation spends 90 percent of their lives indoors, people could not believe it. It was news to them. Thus, the way this Christian spiritual ecology has been woven has created news. To help bring clarity to this work it is now beneficial to clearly state what is going on here in Christian spiritual ecology.

4. Brown, *What Makes You Come Alive*, 60.

First there is the relationship disconnection, which is described by Celtic Christianity as dualism, or in ecotherapy as "the Great Myth." As noted, this disconnection has roots in Christian thinkers like Augustine, with his doctrine of original sin, and in Aristotle's great chain of being. In their own ways, both pivot humanity away from nature. Then there has been the development of our age from the Enlightenment to the modern and current world, which is for the most part secularized. There is also recent research into the continuing habits of the indoor generation and their continued separation from nature. Rather than lay blame on any particular factor behind this separation, it has become clear that this thinking and separation in the relationship with nature has been trending for centuries, which we covered in "Why the Separation?" Because of the long-term development of the trend, the idea is really not on our radar. It is more connected to the progression of time and the advancements of humanity than anything else. As result of this long-term progression we are noticeably numb or indifferent to the natural world and a creator God, if such is one's belief. This is the news in essence from this research: As a current culture and society, we are living an existence that is becoming completely separated from the natural world.

In sum, I have defined the relationship with nature in this work as Christian spiritual ecology. If we break this term down in meaning, "Christian" refers to a belief in a creator God and Jesus as the Author of Life, spirituality to self-realization, and ecology to the study of relationships in nature. This is an expanded definition of the relationship. If I were to write out the information about the relationship as a news headline it might read something like this: *Christians who believe in a creator God and Jesus as the Author of Life are mentally, spiritually, and physically nourished in a relationship with nature.*

There are other headlines that could be applied to this research: e.g., that the way humans relate to the natural world is the greatest contributing factor to global warming. This news and information is out there and for the most part known by our contemporary world. However, we are seeking solutions that perhaps avoid the underlying issue, i.e., that we do not value or practice the human/nature relationship. Just like human-to-human relationships, if we do not tend to them they become damaged. This golden rule to love thy neighbor is found in most world religions, for example, the value of compassion in Buddhism, and so forth. It is also a teaching from Jesus to "love one another as I have loved you." His most important teachings are about tending to relationships. As discussed earlier, the starting point is to love God with all our heart, or in this case, to love nature with all our heart in the ecological relationship. We are better as Christians at loving our neighbor, while the part about loving God/nature with all our heart is all but forgotten. We are ignoring the most crucial point Jesus makes about our relationships.

There is a calling from Jesus to take on the task of teaching about the ecological relationship so as to retain our saltiness, and to be the light. This is not intended as some kind of drudgery. It is instead an epiphany for the contemporary world in that we have almost completely lost this relationship, and we are also losing our own self-understanding as spiritual beings who were created to relate with nature.

The other exciting point about Christian spiritual ecology is that it is not a doctrine, theology, or even a hope. It is a factual reality in light of current scientific research. This prompts us as Christians to go forward in the new way of living without looking back. The gift from Thurman is that "nature is a balm for the soul that seeks reconciliation and wholeness. Seeing manifestations of sacred unity everywhere is a powerful gift we can receive whenever we go outside."[5] Thus, part of the "Where do we go from here?" is an awakening. So what would it look like if we as Christians were to awaken to the value of the ecological relationship?

I personally imagine such an awakening as an opening, a bit like venturing from the doorways of our inside worlds into the natural world. An interesting ecological vision found in the Jewish celebration of Sukkot is found in a passage by Ellen Bernstein in *Ecology and the Jewish Spirit*:

5. Brown, *What Makes You Come Alive*, 60.

> The root of ecology—*ecos*—means "house" in Greek. Ecology understands the earth as home; it is the study of the web of relationships that contribute to the earth's hospitality. This finding was all the more timely given that the Jewish harvest holiday of Sukkot was just around the corner. Sukkot is undeniably the earth's holiday and the time to remember that the true meaning of home is "earth."[6]

Ellen Bernstein goes on to describe the holiday: "Sukkot—as harvest holiday—first teaches that life is intimately tied to the cycle of nature. The holiday assumes that we are ecologists, that we know the species and habitat of our home, and that we participate in the life of our ecosystem."[7] She then describes the Sukkot structure itself:

> The sukkah, the simple open-air hut we build to remember our holiday, had its origin in the temporary structures the Israelites built to shelter their harvest. Living far from the fields, they constructed sheds to protect freshly harvested fruits and vegetables until they were able to transport the crops home. The Torah obligates us to build a sukkah from materials of nature; we are directed to make it beautiful with choice fruits and herbs and to eat and sleep there for seven days. We are also told to invite guests and to share all the bounty and joy with friends and neighbors and those less fortunate.

She concludes with the notion of Sukkot as an ecological vision: "Today, the symbol of the sukkah might serve as the logo for an environmental organization. During this week-long camp-out, we cannot help but learn that the earth is home and the only true shelter is under God's wing. The pleasures of life come from the things we most often take for granted: good food, straight from the earth; good friends; and fresh air. This is a lesson we must learn

6. Bernstein, *Ecology and the Jewish Spirit*, 133.

7. Bernstein, *Ecology and the Jewish Spirit*, 133.

time and again."[8] This is an ecological vision of awakening to our true home: the natural world.

Interestingly, this vision can also be found in the way Japanese structures are built as described by Qing Li in *Forest Bathing*: "Nature is not separate from mankind in Japanese culture. It is part of us. And the need to keep the two in harmony can be seen in every aspect of life, from the design of gardens that incorporate the natural landscape to the design of houses that blur inside and outside by means of translucent paper screens. In traditional Japanese houses you can close the door without shutting out the sound of the birds singing or the rustle of the breeze."[9] This ecological thinking and thread takes us back to the idea of balance and harmony in our human/nature relationship. Christian spiritual ecology is encouragement for that relationship and needed balance in our lives. Awakening to the vision gives rise to endless possible ways of finding harmony and balance with nature. It is not only about having time to be outside; it is also about seriously looking at the way we live, from our homes to our transportation and to the food we eat.

The endless possibilities include how one cultivates time in nature. The practice of forest bathing gives us a very practical and inclusive way for people to spend time in nature. Opening up to this time can be as simple as watching a sunrise or sunset. We might think that time needs to be spent on some grand camping trip or vacation. However, nature is right here every day. Learning from Japanese culture and the Jewish Sukkot, the task is how do we peel away our indoor layer that has become 90 percent of our lives? This need not be treacherous or difficult. This is part of the healing in the relationship in that nature gives us a physical and mental ability to relax. Something to think about when cultivating time for nature is that our current society is not set up for it because it is not something we value. It will thus take effort to create that space and time. In the "Nature of Americans" national report, the research, which is based on the biophilia hypothesis, outlines five reasons

8. Bernstein, *Ecology and the Jewish Spirit*, 133.

9. Qing, *Forest Bathing*, 22.

why our indoor generation is having a difficult time spending time in nature. These are a built-up environment, competing priorities, declining direct dependence, a rise in technology and electronic media, and shifting expectations.[10] The importance of realizing this and how our current world operates is because when these built-in features are left alone, we have little encouragement to heal the relationship.

This is part of the newness and awakening: realizing the need to cultivate this relationship with nature, we are empowered in our church and personal lives to live in ways that develop the relationship. No longer is going outside a pastime. It is a vitally important part of our lives.

To conclude the answer to "Where do we go from here?" let us remind ourselves of the encouragement for this awakening: the twofold benefits of self-realization for the Christian church and individual Christians, and the twofold benefit of healing humanity and healing nature. To begin with the self-realization of church and individual, it is in Muir's words "to become part and parcel of nature" and "a free bit of everything."[11] For our churches now have the language and resources to freely encourage the human/nature relationship. Rather than awkwardly talking in metaphors and theories about God in creation, we can now realize our churches as places in the community to bring about awareness of the need for the human/nature relationship. On a Sunday we now have the language to say the way we relate to nature is a way of relating to God. Our churches are places where the forgotten song of the relationship can now be freely sung out, although perhaps in new versions. In our own personal Christian lives this self-realization can bloom in as many directions as there are Christians. We might imagine the possible works of art, music, and architecture on this topic alone.

And finally, the reason why it is so important for us as Christians to practice and preach about this relationship is because we know of the twofold healing benefits for nature and humanity.

10. US Fish and Wildlife Service, "New Study."

11. Flinders, *John Muir*, 25–26.

While I covered extensively the healing benefits for humanity, I did not say a lot about the healing benefits for nature. This section was more of a nod to the intelligence of nature and advocacy to listen to her wisdom. We established with research from NASA, which is also supported by the UN, that the human relationship is the greatest contributing factor to global warming.[12] The question becomes "Does healing the human/nature ecological relationship contribute to the healing of nature and balance the way we humans relate to nature?" While more research is needed on this topic, an article published in the National Library of Medicine, edited by Soumya Mazumdar, and entitled "Time Spent in Nature Is Associated with Increased Pro-Environmental Attitudes and Behaviors," presents findings affirming that healing the relationship can lead to the healing of nature. "Substantial evidence from observational and intervention studies indicates that overall time spent in nature is associated with increased perceived value for and connection to nature and, subsequently, greater PEAB."[13] "PEAB" stands for "Pro-Environmental Attitudes and Behaviors." And there we have it. Valuing this relationship is incredibly important in our current times in light of our environmental crisis.

Let us pause and breathe for a little while here.

What happened to us as Christians? I believe we overthought this whole thing in our theologies. There is nothing wrong with any past theologians as individuals and Christians; it is just that they overthought and theorized God away from nature. And we have built our churches on this kind of thinking and have told indigenous religions it is wrong to worship God in nature.

Because, like Thurman and Muir, I have been baptized in nature; when I hear Christians confusing the narrative about the human/nature relationship, it saddens me. We need to admit Christianity has really struggled with this relationship and at times has made it seem wrong. We need to move forward into a Christianity that simply nourishes the relationship with nature. There is a point being made here in this research that it is our Christian

12. United Nations, "What Is Climate Change?"

13. National Library of Medicine, "Time in Nature."

theology of the past and our overthinking of the relationship that is problematic. They are self-fulfilling prophecies in that we get consumed by human thought to the point where God and Jesus are removed from the picture. That is the teaching from Genesis and the garden of Eden, in which the tree of knowledge of good and evil warns us not to think we are like God, because doing so removes God from the relationship. There is another tree in the garden called the tree of life, which in Judaic study is about the spiritual relationship with a living God.

Concerning the problematic tendency to overthink in theology, there is an interesting article titled "Christianity and Ecology" from the Yale Forum on Religion and Ecology. In the article there are essay references from a group of eighty Christian scholars on the topic of Christian ecology from Cambridge, Massachusetts, in 1998. The group points out the problems in our past Christian thinking: "Christian theology played a key role in ecological and cultural malformation by giving impetus to the modern, rational, scientific conquest of nature."[14]

It stops short of advocating for the relationship with a final statement from Rosemary Radford Ruether's concluding essay on "the centrality of eco-justice in authentic Christian witness. For Ruether, this is not a new or marginal emphasis for Christian life and thought; rather, it is central to a full understanding of the church's mission as witness to and participant in God's redemption of creation."[15]

We are right back where we started, the notion that creation is in need of redemption and human beings, as better and more intelligent, are the ones to redeem it. Here again there is nothing wrong with this group of people who are concerned about the environment. The problem is that continued overthinking removes God and Jesus from nature, and as Christians, we have all fallen for it.

Because of this overthinking and worship of the human mind and human intelligence, we need to get over ourselves. I made an

14. Yale Forum on Religion and Ecology, "Christianity Introduction."

15. Yale Forum on Religion and Ecology, "Christianity Introduction."

appeal to humility in the section on healing nature. If we have ever experienced the healing aspect of nature, and in Muir's words become a "free bit of everything,"[16] we return to the world not thinking that as humans we are smarter than God or nature. Our minds are freed to see the magnificence of God's creation. This importance of humility in our natural spirituality is explained in *The Book of Joy*. The word "humility" itself has roots in the word *humus* meaning "soil" or "earth":

> The Dalai Lama and the Archbishop were both insistent that humility is essential to any possibility of joy. When we have a wider perspective, we have a natural understanding of our place in the great sweep of all that was, is, and will be. This naturally leads to humility and the recognition that as human beings we can't solve everything or control all aspects of life. We need others. The Archbishop has poignantly said that our vulnerabilities, our frailties, and our limitations are a reminder that we need one another: We are not created for independence or self-sufficiency, but for interdependence and mutual support.[17]

This tendency for us as humans to become consumed by our own intelligence and independence has led to the point where we have created a world where we live 90 percent of our time separated from a life-giving God and natural world. This can be healed by realizing our natural interdependence and the humility of that.

The intention of this work is for Christians to move past a theology of the human/nature relationship into a spiritual ecology that is the actual practice of the relationship. We can then use the latest scientific and historical research to support the practice of this spiritual ecological relationship. Our findings are first, that as a current society we are increasingly not practicing this relationship, leading to a growing distance between the human and natural worlds. Second, the healing aspects of this relationship in our findings are that there is need and benefit for us as Christians

16. Flinders, *John Muir*, 26–27.

17. Dalai Lama and Tutu, *Book Of Joy*, 208–9.

to practice this ecological relationship by spending more time in nature. As called for in the alignment of our beliefs and the sciences, we can now confidently move forward as Christians into the practice of this new Christian spiritual ecology.

Chapter 8: The Spiritual Practice

> "God is spirit, and his worshipers must worship in the Spirit and in truth." (John 4:24)

TAKING THE TIME

One thing our investigation into the separation between humanity and nature teaches us is that it takes effort in our current world to spend time in nature, unlike former farming or hunter-gathering cultures where the time spent was simply the way of life. These days we have to consciously create the time in our lives to do so. While technology does make it easier for us to not spend time in nature, it can also help us. If we meet virtually for a class or meeting, for example, we can generate spare time from not having to travel to the physical location of the meeting. Depending on our individual situations, there will always be creative ways to use technology to free up time.

Prioritizing time is also important. Throughout my life of being drawn to God and the natural world I often did not make money in doing so, and so I often felt guilty about the time spent. In a world based on a forty-hour work week and time schedules, it felt as if I was being unproductive. This is not to say one cannot have a nine-to-five job and still create time for nature every day. But if we let society convince us spending time in nature is a waste of time or nonproductive, we will find ourselves giving it less priority. One of the foundational things to remember in prioritizing such time is in the mental and physical health benefits of being in nature. If we are feeling better mentally and physically, we will tend to be more productive when we are at work. There is thus a compelling reason why the time should be prioritized every day.

The regularity of every day is also essential. Granted there may be days where one is traveling or a schedule is so full it is not possible. However, having a practice of creating time for nature every day is essential. Take any other practice, such as playing a musical instrument. If one practices just once in a while the practice and the music will suffer. It is the same with this spiritual practice: learning from Mother Nature is much like learning a musical instrument.

Depending on one's individual background, prioritizing time will look different. One thing to note is that the other things that take up our daily time will need to be evaluated. Perhaps ways we lived before will need to change. In surfing culture, surfers tend to live simple and productive lives in order to have time to surf every day. Because surfing becomes the center of one's life, other demands on one's time become secondary or even omitted if not necessary for a healthy life.

Last, Christians prioritizing such time are following Jesus' teaching to love God with all our hearts. To take time from our busy schedules to celebrate a relationship with a living creator God is to practice this greatest commandment from Jesus. In an increasingly secular world, it is a natural opportunity to center oneself on a relationship with God. The importance of centering our lives in God leads into the next section on the humility and service associated with the practice.

HUMILITY AND SERVICE

It would sound ironic if I were to say I am the most humble person there is. And thus often we don't speak of humility, and think of it only as an action, and an action anyone with humility would not want you to talk about. However, in the relationship with Jesus,

God, and nature, humility is a spiritual practice. Part of its importance is it takes us out of the material world we have built. As described in the account of the separation from nature, we live in a built world that separates us from the natural world. What this creates in the human consciousness is the belief that, as humans, we are creating our own existence. We go to the grocery store to obtain food, and other materials for our homes and lives. It has been removed from our consciousness that all these things actually come from God and the natural world. Humility helps us remove this material shell. Humility has within it the practice of gratitude that Jesus teaches. To give thanks is a way of blessing our lives and helping us realize where our provisions are really from.

In *The Book of Joy*, we discover we have become so bound to the material world we have lost our own spirituality. To focus on our own breath is what the word "spirit" means. To breathe into our souls and simplify our lives in that practice of humility connects us to the Holy Spirit and natural world while slowing down the material world. As we learned from the benefits of spending time in nature, our bodies and minds experience that spiritual, meditative slowing down.

This does not mean that we have to live with nothing. What humility and gratefulness do is help us realize what we essentially need for a good life and for spirituality. Our material needs will alter in order that we might allow ourselves to have more time in nature. For each individual this will look different. Interestingly we may find some of the material things we thought we needed are actually keeping us away from this spiritual practice and a healthy life.

What humility also offers is a chance learn from nature. As described in "Taking the Time," much like learning an instrument, the more time one spends in nature, the more she will teach us. Throughout the ages nature has taught and inspired humanity in what we create and construct. From Velcro to wetsuits and to airplane design, the wisdom of nature can be found to have functioned as a teacher. I can share an example from my own work in constructing this book. As I was looking to turn my doctoral research into a manuscript, I had a dream one night about a spider web. The next day I tried to figure out how a spider makes a web with that empty circle at the center. I felt understanding this might teach me something about constructing my manuscript. I could not figure out the construction and so began watching time-lapse videos of spiders making webs. What I learned is that in the beginning they have lines of silk crisscrossing in the center in an "X" pattern. From there they create circles around the "X" pattern, and then they return to the circle and eat out the silk in the center circle. So, I returned to this book with a new vision of the construction. I asked myself, "Where is the center, and how do I remove something from the center?" What I realized was there was the need for a center between the definition of spiritual ecology, descriptions of the early pioneers, and enumeration of the benefits and this later section on the spiritual practice. That center was "Why the Separation?" which was interestingly, and metaphorically, like the spider removing the "X" from the inner circle of its web. The section on reasons for the separation performed the same function in terms of identifying how humanity has removed time spent in nature from our culture. I could then move on to look at ways of bridging the separation in the next section of togetherness. Not only did this understanding from nature help me see how to put this book together, it also created a space for the Spirit to flow through.

Humility does not mean we have to be less of a person. It is more about realizing the teaching of God in nature through the Holy Spirit, which in turn will help us fully realize ourselves in the sense of oneness with creation. Humility as a practice also allows us to take the burden from our shoulders to realize we are not alone and allow a living God into our lives who teaches us through Jesus about service.

> "Therefore, I tell you, do not worry about your life, what you will eat or drink; or about your body, what you will wear. Is not life more than food, and the body more than clothes? Look at the birds of the air; they do not sow or reap or store away in barns, and yet your heavenly Father feeds them. Are you not much more valuable than they?

> Can any one of you by worrying add a single hour to your life?" (Matthew 6:25–27)

The Beatitudes of Jesus and his response to his disciples' questions about who is the greatest embody this teaching of humility and service to God and others. He tells us we cannot serve two things at once. A life serving God gives us clarity about our priorities and what is important in our lives. That, I believe, is the point Jesus is making in these teachings. It is not that we should not have material goods or money. It is more that through serving God we learn how to share more of that loving light in the world that has to do with concern for God, creation, ourselves, and our neighbors. It may come about through the giving of material provisions. However, the point and focus are rather than only focusing on the material world, we realize God's presence in the material world. We can think of Jesus' command to give, which flips the script of our perceptions of the material world and our possessions, because the requirement is instead to store up treasure in heaven. Our treasure in heaven is where our heart is. A heart of love is a practice of living with God's love and sharing that love with the world.

The idea that love is not a competition is something that Jesus is teaching us. The material world is one of haves and have-nots, which at times gets competitive. This teaching from Jesus is about realizing the abundant love of a creator God and sharing that with the world, which leads to our next section on the fruits of the practice of ecological spirituality.

THE FRUITS OF THE PRACTICE

Jesus often draws on examples from nature to describe eternal life on earth and relationship with him. He also often describes it as a fruit. For example, he says: "I am the vine, you are the branches. If you remain in me and I in you, you will bear much fruit" (John 15:5). He also likens following him to tending to a field of crops with one's hand on the plow and so forth. Being spiritually fed by time spent in nature is a fruit we can speak of. We do not think of it in this way often, but time spent in nature is literally a time of worship. The result of spending time in nature is the same as leaving church spiritually filled. It is just that as Christians, we have not allowed ourselves to say that. It is my view that our disconnectedness from nature has the same effect as ceasing to go to church and worship God there. So not only are we ignoring a living God in creation, we also are missing out on being fed spiritually and daily in that relationship. The fruit of being spiritually fed is available in the ecological relationship, which builds a relationship with Jesus and God. We have been taught this happens in church and perhaps when we are out serving others, yet there is a far more expansive relationship available to add to our church and serving times.

I have spoken of the cognitive and physical benefits from the time spent in nature, which is an obvious fruit of doing so. However, there is also fruit for creation itself. As with any relationship, when we begin relating with God and Jesus in nature we begin to understand what it is God needs in the natural world. At this point we can better understand how to take care of creation.

If the fruit of our relationship with nature comes from sharing our heart-centered love of God with others and the world, the yield is an endless and eternal abundance. It is a fruit that expands in much the same way as the mustard seed or the yeast in bread Jesus talks about when explaining the kingdom of heaven. Planting a tree, carbon footprint-ing, helping a neighbor have access to clean water, buying non-processed foods, and having a pollinator garden all reflect love for the natural world and others in the sense of caring for God and one another. What ecological spirituality teaches us is how we live our lives has an impact on creation and others. This is also the teaching of process thinking from folks like John Cobb, in that the process of our interactions is a process of relation to a living creator God.

As in Jesus' parable of the sower, the seed that does well in good soil is seed sown in the heart. This heart-centered approach results in fruit because we are not distracted by material things and the worries of the world. The ecological relationship simply means that we are relating to God, Jesus, and the natural world. This leads to the fruit of becoming one with God, Jesus, and creation, and seeing possibilities that are often limited in the material world. In terms of spiritual growth, this ecology offers growth in care for one another and for the environment.

THE BALANCE

As mentioned before, I believe the Lord's Prayer is fitting for any pastoral situation because it is a prayer of balance and calls for the presence of our heavenly Creator with us in relationship. The prayer starts by looking towards the sanctity of God and then asking that the eternal Creator's presence be realized within creation, in God's will being "done on earth as in heaven" (Matt 6:10). The prayer then gives thanks for the daily provisions given to us by creation. Next, the prayer asks for a balance of forgiveness and help resisting the temptation to move away from relationship with God. The Christian spiritual ecology advocated here is also about promoting that relationship. When we look back at theories and doctrines such as the great chain of being or original sin, they seem very unbalanced in nature, for in them, humanity and nature are separated and the relationship is thrown out of balance.

This unbalanced relationship is harmful to humanity, as we have learned, but also to creation itself, with both NASA and the UN confirming the greatest contributing factor to our environmental crisis is how we as humans relate to the natural world. The core problem of what we are currently facing is the ecological relationship itself. As in any relationship, if one party ignores the needs of the other, the result is going to be an unhealthy relationship. And that is exactly what is happening right now with our indoor generation.

This is not to claim that Christian spiritual ecology can solve the world's problems. However, becoming aware how unbalanced our relationship with nature is right now is a step in the right direction. In the sense of a spiritual practice, this can be unfolded in as many ways as there are individuals. All of our moments of self-realization will offer a balance to this relationship. The example that I practice from my own ministry setting is advocating for pollinator gardens and creating habitats for pollinators to replace the obsession for turf grass lawns, which have their own environmental impact from the chemicals and treatments used, and the resulting loss of habitat. We have created three large pollinator gardens at our church with a large variety of pollinator plants, along with varieties of milkweed necessary for the survival of the endangered monarch butterfly. Pollinator gardens provide a balance in our yards that offsets the loss of habitat, which is one of the reasons the monarch is endangered.

The monarch butterfly offers its own spiritual gift to the balance, for it is considered a very spiritual creature, and is a reminder of the miracles of God's creation. The transformation from caterpillar to butterfly is also one of the best ways to describe Jesus' resurrection. Amazingly these creatures are born in northern regions with the knowledge to be able to travel south to Mexico to survive the winter and then return to pass that knowledge on to the next generation. They arrive in Mexico around the beginning of the Day of the Dead, which is similar in time and concept to All Saints' Day, with its remembrance of our loved ones now in heaven. The monarchs are believed to represent the return of these spirits, and are seen as a reminder of their presence on earth as it is in heaven.

What all these aspects of the spiritual practice point to is balance: balance in how we spend our time in this relationship daily; the humility to not become so self- and materialistically absorbed that we miss celebrating this relationship; the realization we need spiritual fruit in our days and not just the fruits of our material indoor world. So too is balance reflected in the next section, which is about finding one's true self in nature, a theme which I have been developing in this work.

FINDING OUR TRUE SELVES

When studying the spiritual practices of counseling and so forth, we find there are a lot of archetypical systems upon which to draw and with which to identify. Nature in itself is one of these, in the sense that we may identify with certain parts of creation that help us realize our own personal spiritual selves. There are also self-identifiers that we all can relate to. The Enneagram, for example, has become a popular tool for self-identification. There is nothing wrong with these types of self-identifiers. However, in the case of the ecological spiritual practice, I am speaking of something different. Gandhi, Thurman, and Muir were all very specific when describing self-realization as a way of becoming one with God through creation, or as I have been expressing it, by relating with God and Jesus in nature. The two most common words Jesus himself uses to describe this relationship are "peace" and "love." John 14:27: "Peace I leave you with, my peace I give you. I do not give to you as the world gives. Do not let your heart be troubled and do not be afraid."

This mention of "world" could be interpreted as a reference to the natural world and our earthly existence here; however, as noted earlier, the original Greek word for "world" here is again *cosmos*, with its meaning of "a constitution," or "an ordered arrangement of things." The question then becomes which *cosmos* or "arrangement of things" is Jesus referring to? In the past, many interpreters have assumed "world" here means creation itself. However, if we go back to the teaching of Irenaeus and the notion of Jesus recapitulating the world as the Author of Life, we encounter the possibility Jesus is referring instead to the human world and its relationship to God. As in the parable of the sower, and unlike the good heart-centered soil, he is pointing to a human *cosmos* of worries and distractions.

In the same way we can think of our indoor generation as representing a certain *cosmos* or world, or a currently ordered arrangement of things. The ecological world I am describing is a very different *cosmos*. For spending time in nature lowers our anxiety and gives us peace, as Jesus indicates. This is the peace that frees Thurman from mental subjugation, and the peace from nature where in baptism Muir becomes a free bit of everything. In this understanding, spending time in nature allows us an opportunity to realize our own inner peace.

How self-realized peace and love might look is as individual and varied as there are people in the world. It is often held, with reference to the disciples giving up their fishing trade to follow Jesus, that we too must give up our personal self-realization and instead follow Jesus. Yet the truth, as we discover later in the Gospels, is that the disciples return to their fishing after the resurrection, as John describes Jesus sharing a meal with them after they have been out fishing. It thus makes more sense to understand self-realization as gaining a certain world-understanding by following Jesus and loving God with all our heart. Doing so will then lead to the fruit of finding peace in our lives while being better able to fulfill our own personal passions, along with our service.

The same can be said about Jesus teaching us about a loving God. We are to love one another as he has loved us. We are to love our neighbors as ourselves. This points to a self-realization of love that we are encouraged to share with others. Have we ever heard nature say a harmful word? Has nature ever judged anyone? Does nature hold grudges and not forgive? The obvious answer to these questions is no. I suggest this to help us realize just how loving Mother Nature is. Often, after time spent in nature, I think to myself I would rather not be returning because the experience has been as loving as being in heaven. Just being in a space that is entirely uncritical is a soothing balm for the soul.

The self-realization that Gandhi speaks of is connected to realizing the essential oneness of life through nonviolence. In other words, in becoming one with a loving God through nature one is filled with love to the point that violence becomes absurd, and to not love something or someone no longer makes sense. In some cultures we might refer to this as "being enlightened." As O. E. Wilson proposes, apart from nature our lives have little meaning, in the sense that the meaning we find is that we are loved by God, which we then reflect back to the world.[1] Becoming that free bit of everything Muir speaks of means becoming one with a creator God in the loving *cosmos* God has created.

1. Wilson, *Biophilia*, 82.

CULTURE

We learned from the statistics about the indoor generation that our culture does not value spending time in the natural world. This is not something intentional, but something that has happened over time almost imperceptibly and unthinkingly. This is all the more reason for us to develop a conscious practice, because this is not something that is likely to be encouraged by our culture. Here again, depending on our lifestyle, job situation, family life, and so forth, this will look different for each of us. I do believe in tending to the elements of this practice (time, humility, fruits, balance, and self-realization) will enable us to find a way to cultivate this relationship with nature in our contemporary culture.

Surfing culture reveals that because time spent surfing is usually the center of a surfer's practice, that person will structure their life in such a way as to have the time available to do so when the surf is up. Depending on one's vocation, this might take some creativity, especially if the waves are out there on a Monday morning. From a sociological understanding, we are aware that what a society or culture values will dictate how it operates and lives. So, the lesson implied here is that placing a value on spending time in nature in an ecological relationship will begin to shift the very culture.

We do not necessarily have to be countercultural. I envision this process more as letting our culture shift towards the value of spending time in nature. Because of the inclusivity of the practice, which tends to the individual spirit regardless of cultural background, there should be the ability to shift any culture towards valuing time spent in nature. A tree does not produce its oxygen and aroma for any one particular culture. We all deserve to be in receipt of that value. Centering our own personal culture on the ecological relationship is just the same. For example, there is no reason why a businessperson who loves the stock market and so forth cannot entertain that passion as well as a passion for ecological practice. This is the freedom and fun of this practice. People and cultures do not have to lose their identities simply because they have shifted their focus and centered it around the practice of ecological spirituality.

THANKFULNESS AND GIVING

> "Bring them here to me," he said. And he directed the people to sit down on the grass. Taking the five loaves and the two fish and looking up to heaven, he gave thanks and broke the loaves. Then he gave them to the disciples, and the disciples gave them to the people. (Matthew 14:18–19)

As noted previously, Jesus encourages us to store up treasure in heaven rather than focus on wealth and material possessions. This treasure is that which is close to our hearts and which brings us happiness and abundance. It enables us to realize our creator God truly is a giver in all the things we need. Jesus teaches in relationship to a creator God that we are also to become givers in the world. Giving can take many forms: time, talents, and materials. However, as a spiritual practice, our treasure in heaven is a realization of the gift of life, the awareness that creation is from God, and our thankfulness for that. In my opinion, when we consider that the greatest contributing factor to the environmental crisis is the human/nature relationship, the root of our problem is that there is far more taking from nature than giving.

As Christians we have a good understating of what it is to give to one another. Here we might think of all the different food drives and outreaches from churches designed to care for the community. Giving to God and to creation is typically a secondary consideration. If we are to love God with all our hearts, is it not important to also give to creation itself? There are many practical ways to do so. My own personal practice of creating pollinator habitats makes the spiritual practice of giving a living thing and not just a policy. It means giving our time to be with God and Jesus in nature, listening to her daily, and observing her movements and teachings. From the sense of oneness this brings, we find ourselves refreshed and more able to give to others and nature.

The abundance teaching from Jesus in the narratives of the loaves and the fishes, and his words about storing up treasure in heaven, are all about this practice of giving. Take for example the parables of seeds, such as the parable of the sower and the parable of the mustard seed. These teachings also reflect the abundantly giving nature of creation and God. In Ps 65, it is written, "The streams of God are filled with water to provide the people with grain, for so you have ordained it." Here we have a literal description of God's presence in the abundance-giving aspect of nature that Jesus teaches about in relation to almsgiving also. Giving is a spiritual practice. God is a giver, Jesus is a giver, and the natural world is a giver. The treasure stored up in heaven comes from giving from our hearts in relation with God and Jesus.

In his sermon to the birds, St. Francis warns them against the sin of ingratitude, as God has given them everything they need, including their own lives. Being grateful leads naturally to giving as we see in Jesus giving thanks for the fish and loaves. All these aspects of the spiritual practice are things we can live out in our lives. Daily being grateful for what we have, including being alive, creates an attitude of abundance and giving. In the sense of the ecological relationship with God, Jesus, nature, and humanity, the essence of the relationship is one of giving. Here again past theories, such as the great chain of being, which places humanity as superior, trick us into thinking we are the ones creating our daily provision instead of the reality, which is that all of life is a gift from a living God. However, being an indoor generation, lacking an awareness of the natural world and its provision, leads us to unawareness of our need to be grateful, because we have lost the perception of where all our life-giving resources are truly from.

PRAYER AND OUR PERCEPTION OF THE NATURAL WORLD

When our society looks out at the natural world, it sees a tree that can be turned into lumber, water that can be consumed, and land that can be altered for farms and construction sites. The paradigm shift in the practice I am advocating is to begin to perceive the natural world as a space in which to be with God and the Holy Spirit of Jesus' resurrection. While there have been various Christian thinkers who have compared the natural world to a church, we need to move that concept forward and affirm nature is not only a place of worship but also a classroom in which to learn from God, a place of spiritual journey where we find ourselves, a place for natural meditation that gives differently from our humanly constructed world, and a place of abundance as described in the Bible. There are many more things the reader could add here. The point, however, is that our human material perception limits our possibilities of relating with God in nature, and that numerous opportunities could be created from a changed perception.

There is movement of God in the rain and sunshine, along with a response from plants. However, we as humans have become so self-absorbed we do not pay attention to this. The main characteristic of the indoor generation is a focus on the self, to the point where we believe it is humans who produce food, which we do by going to the store or ordering a delivery. We are so removed from the ecological relationship with nature and God we no longer perceive it. The obvious change in perception being described here is to spend the time in nature to gain awareness of this ordained presence of God and Jesus in the natural world. Through prayer and thanksgiving we can also change our perception that the gifts of life are from a creator God. It sounds like a simple thing, but it is what Jesus does in the multiplication of the loaves and fishes. Prayer, like all the other features of this spiritual practice, is a practice in itself. It reminds us that whatever is before us is a gift from God. While it might seem as if we made the money and then went out and bought the things we need, everything is instead truly from the living God.

Prayer is open communication with God and Jesus. Being in nature is a resoundingly peaceful prayer. I will say that again: being in nature is a resoundingly peaceful prayer in which we are relating ecologically with Jesus and God. This is a vastly different perception from that of our fast-paced culture speeding off into the future. In my opinion we are speeding away from the meaning of life, which is to relate to God and one another in loving and giving ways. We chase after this and that, all the while further distancing ourselves from God and nature. Yet right before us is this beautiful, peaceful prayer waiting for us outside in nature, completely free, but we are not perceiving it; we have stopped perceiving it.

ADVOCATING FROM ONENESS AND CREATING PEACEFUL SPACE

Christians are familiar with the phrase "in the world but not of it" which comes from the Gospel of John. It has been interpreted to mean Jesus and his followers have a heavenly or divine presence in comparison to the world. This understanding is actually similar to Gnosticism, which the early Christian bishops struggled against, and which led to the formulation of popular creeds affirming the humanity of Jesus.

That gnostic interpretation of the saying also fits in neatly with the concept of original sin. We then say the world is bad, and full of sin, but that we as Christians have been freed from sin and are not part of that world. The problem with this understanding is that here the word "world" is interpreted much like our English word for "world" with its meaning of the natural earth itself. But discussed in the earlier section on cosmology, understanding the original Greek word for "world" in these texts is again *cosmos*, which means "the way things are ordered." This shifts the meaning away from the natural world towards the way humanity exists in the world.

Once again this makes more sense of what Jesus means when he says, "I do not give as the world gives" (John 14:27). He would then be talking about *cosmos* in the sense of humanity's way of judgment, hate, and violence, compared to his teachings of almsgiving, forgiveness, and loving ourselves, God and neighbor. This very world we have described as the natural world is a place that gives and teaches us about giving.

So, when we say "be not of the world" we are not talking about oneness of the world through ecological relationship, but rather the world of the human, with all its materialism, violence, and so forth. For me, this is literally a perception or awareness I have whenever I return from surfing or spending a good amount of time in nature. When your mind is refreshed you feel a sense of peace and calm, but when you enter back into society, it seems very strange and foreign, for it is a world that is different than the natural world.

It is a spiritual practice in itself to remain in the peace and self-understanding of oneness with which we return from nature and not compromise it with the human world (much as the distractions of the world in the parable of the sower interfere with the growth of the seed). We also need to be able to create spaces of peace and to teach about its giving aspects. I have noticed in my studies that at times ecologists and those working on environmental advocacy find themselves in such opposition to the materially constructed human world, and so frustrated that they end up losing the peaceful experience and spiritual practice of ecology. As an ecologist, I believe it is important for us to teach peace and to offer that peace to the world rather than to be in opposition to the world. And we all have the ability to practice this type of spiritual ecology.

Remaining in love and a heart-centered practice teaches others that a living God of nature loves them as well. Taking a fighting stance only creates resistance. This teaching of peace and interconnectedness is found throughout the natural world. We just have to think about the process of photosynthesis, water cycles with the sun, and so on. An ecology of relationship teaches us about interconnectedness and inclusion. It makes sense then to practice this in our spirituality, for it also aligns with Jesus' teaching of love and forgiveness.

MYRIAD INDIVIDUAL ECOLOGIES AND COMMUNITIES

I hope this is a starting point for you, and that you can enter your ecological practice as a Christian with a sense of celebration. However much diversity there is in each individual faith, only Jesus and God truly know the myriad of personal faiths out there. So, this ecological practice will vary depending on you as an individual. Maybe you are a landscape artist, and your ecological practice is spending large amounts of time creating beautiful paintings or photos. The point here is about putting your own unique stamp on this practice. Have fun. Don't take yourself too seriously, for that adds to the humility of the practice. Be safe. Know your own personal limits while learning about yourself out there.

The ecological community is going to become increasingly important given our present environmental concerns. We need to find a way each individual ecological practice can help inform the community so that there might be a change in this generation with all its time spent indoors. Changing our perceptions about our ecological relationship with nature will lead to better environmental practices. The pandemic taught us that when humanity slowed down, the environment began to be less polluted. So, taking time out of our day, and instead of creating pollution, taking a walk in the fresh air, will have its own effects. For some reason humans have evolved into being content with life being an indoor affair. We seem content with our human selves, all the while omitting God and the natural world from our community.

True community in my opinion includes the natural world to the point where it teaches us about community and ecological relationships. The natural world teaches us to give and help one another out. It is a place of unconditional love. The hope is, in our individual ecological practices, we can begin pondering different possibilities of community relationships in which the natural is considered part of our community.

WHEN NATURE IS NO LONGER THE OTHER

Living in ecological relationship with nature and becoming who we are as Christians is a way of life. This can now be our identity. We are people of the earth, much as Genesis describes God breathing life into clay. We can get over the separation narrative, which is something the environmental crisis is crying out for us to do. We began with a definition of ecology as the study of relationships. So too I believe Jesus' teachings are very centered on relationships. The task of loving God with all our heart and loving our neighbors as ourselves is essentially a focus on relationships.

When we think of the parable of the good Samaritan and stories about Jesus healing on the sabbath, the message is about giving grace and compassion to the other. When nature is no longer the other and becomes part of our relationship with God and Jesus, we are compelled to realize how our lives are sustained and blessed by the natural world. This in turn leads our own compassion to treat nature in the same way. No longer is it a material resource from which we get our daily needs to support our indoor lives. Instead, it is the lovely living God Jesus teaches us about.

So, when nature is no longer the other, God is no longer the other either. One more time: when nature is no longer the other, God is no longer the other. This is oneness. Jesus as described by John is within all creation, since the beginning of creation supports that relationship in our own personal relationship with him. In the ecological relationship, Jesus and God are in the spiritual air we breathe into our souls. Past Christian theologies that separate Jesus and God from the natural world, or that perceive nature as less intelligent, no longer make any sense.

Relationships are all about supporting one another. This teaching is all over the ecosystems of the natural world. We begin to see our daily decisions have an effect on the natural world once we realize how it gives to us and nourishes us daily. The core problem, as we have learned from the environmental crisis, is the human/nature relationship. Think of any healthy relationship you have encountered and the mutual support found there. Because we have become so disconnected from nature, as humans we do not support her. It is that simple. Becoming one and finding ourselves in nature will cultivate a culture of care for her.

Sadly, our indoor generation is living a life where the natural world and God are the other. This indifference to the natural world does have spiritual implications. Besides the loss of health, in my opinion the indoor generation is experiencing also a spiritual loss. It is a culture that has lost its way in relating with a creator God. However, teaching about spiritual ecology and the relationship with nature can create awareness of this loss.

The awareness that we must not allow the natural world to be the other is the ingredient needed here. We have slowly and unconsciously created our indoor world. If we do not change our perspective, very little will happen. However, if we are willing to change our perspective and realize the spiritual loss of not having a relationship with God, Jesus, and the natural world, change in individual lives and benefits to the environment will become possible. This awareness is basically a change in attitudes and values. We have all experienced changes of perspectives in our lives, maybe through the loss of a loved one, hearing a hymn sung on a Sunday, the reminder of ashes on Ash Wednesday, taking communion, or perhaps a teacher giving us a new understanding. A paradigm shift occurs when we think our world is composed a certain way but then receive a light that shows it is composed by spirit and God.

Distancing ourselves from the natural world is distancing ourselves from God and Jesus. When we think about Jesus and the accounts of him in the Gospels, for the most part they revolve around outdoor natural events. The Sermon on the Mount or Plain, the feeding of loaves and fishes, fishing with the disciples, the place of his transfiguration, baptism in the Jordan, forty days in the wilderness, and more. Once in a while we find him in a temple or speaking with synagogue leaders, but these are not his main places of worship. The natural world is. That is his chosen place to teach and preach about a living God. In his parables, it is the natural world that best explains the kingdom of heaven. In Matt 13:35 Jesus quotes Ps 78:2, saying, "I will open my mouth in parables and utter things hidden since the beginning of creation."

CULTIVATING AN INDIVIDUAL SPIRITUAL PRACTICE

As each of us is uniquely created, this practice will vary from person to person. How much time one has, different interests, finances, and physical abilities will change from individual to individual. The idea about beginning to focus in on and practice this ecology is to realize our oneness with nature, and that it is not the other. This relationship has been there and will be there always; only in our indoor generation we have stopped realizing this. One of the most basic common denominators we all share is how we live through our day. For example, we all need to eat and drink, so right there is an ecological relationship that we can begin with. Here again what we do will vary depending on individual dietary needs and possible restrictions. That saying that we are what we eat is quite true. They way we shop and eat has a direct impact on the environment. In other words there is an immediate spiritual practice we can adopt from a changed perspective, regardless of our lifestyle.

Transportation, housing, and other essential materials are also part of an ecological relationship. While we might not think of it in this way, how we survive day to day is itself an interaction with nature. Obviously, this will vary depending on one's location, financial resources, and so forth. Regardless, like the food we eat, it can become a daily ecological practice to pay attention to our connectedness and the relationship with the natural world in the way that we live.

This said, as with any practice, e.g., hobby, sport, art, or craft, we need to devote our personal time to cultivating it. As with any passion, we learn more about it and develop skills from practice.

This is why it is important to have the time to interact daily with the natural world. The relationship develops as we experience the physical and cognitive benefits of doing so. However, a learning also occurs concerning God, Jesus, and nature. For example, in surfing we find the term "a water person." The idea is that the more time spent interacting with the water the more knowledgeable one becomes about it. The same can be said of a master gardener—someone who has spent years with plants and so understands plant life. So too is the teaching of nature.

Noteworthy in this teaching is awareness of the fresh air and the quiet nature provides. Even in stormy weather, nature provides quietness in contrast to the human world, along with fresh air. On a good surf day, the sound of the waves crashing in fills one's listening space to the point where the words and sounds of the human world fade, which, as we know, produces a cognitive replenishment. It is the same with fresh air. Along with this quietness there is another noteworthy thing that we as Christians seek in nature: the presence of God and Jesus.

In time one notices how different that outdoor space is compared to our human indoor world full of noises and at times seeming chaos. For example, if one returns from time in nature and goes into a grocery store, all of a sudden the world is filled with noises, people chattering, machines ringing, and traffic outside, as well the fresh air disappearing.

It can help us envision the practice by thinking of it as similar to learning to play a musical instrument. When we are in the quietness and fresh air, we become attuned to the environment. The more time we spend with a musical instrument, the more we discover the nuances of its scales, rhythms, and melodies. The practice of the human/nature relationship then has the ability to change and inform our own spiritual lives through self-realization. All things are derived from nature. Science and mathematics are a study of nature, so regardless of one's personal life, passions, and occupation, the time spent in this practice has the ability to help inform and change our lives.

To understand this ecological spiritual practice we can begin with the biblical understanding of the spirit as breath and air. In a simple sense, this practice is really a focus on our spirits and how we breathe through our day in relationship with Mother Nature, God, and Jesus. Like a meditation or quiet time of prayer, the busyness of the human world is quieted, enabling a calming focus on our breath and ourselves as lovingly created by God from nature.

There are many perspectives on the Holy Spirit, including the prevailing one of the Spirit as part of the Trinity along with the Father and the Son. I find it interesting that in the Gospel of John, John the Baptist talks of Jesus baptizing with the Holy Spirit. In our relationship with him, he is that Holy Spirit within all creation "without whom nothing was made that has been made," as stated in the Gospel (John 1:3).

When one studies spirituality as I have defined it here, our spirit is the individual personality of our souls. The Holy Spirit is the imprint of Jesus, and in that loving relationship with him, we are taught about a loving creator God. We each then in our own lives have our own spirits that make us unique as individuals in the way God created us. When we look towards nature the same can be said. Water for example has a very specific spiritual identity. It cleanses, has the ability to take different forms, makes up most of our bodies, is essential for life, and has a very life-giving aspect. Many of these characteristics are a significant reason for water being used in baptism. Trees, birds, insects, sunlight, animals, and plants also all have individual spiritual traits and teachings.

In our study of ecology and relationships, we realize in a relationship sense how we are connected to these other spirits, just as we would say we have a relationship with Jesus as our friend and the Holy Spirit. The stories about Saint Francis are a fine example of this as he interacts with nature the Holy Spirit in the same way.

Just as each of us have individual personality traits, we also have personal preferences as to what these spiritual relationships might be. Perhaps someone likes the rain and redwoods, for example. Different individuals are drawn to particular landscapes because of individual preferences. It is the same with the plants, animals, birds, and other ecosystems. So, there is really no right or wrong in the way of self-realization amidst the aspects of nature in which the Holy Spirit encourages our spiritual filling and growth. I am fascinated by and love monarch butterflies. I remember their abundance in the summertime out in nature as a child. As mentioned, recently I have been creating pollinator habitats for them at our churches, for they are currently on the endangered species list. They also happen to provide a wonderful way of describing Jesus' resurrection. As Christians, we do not realize God's forgiveness, grace, and love, then through Jesus we are saved and realize God through him, and like the monarch, are thus transformed. This is an example of spiritual teaching from the monarch's own unique spirit.

From the Christian perspective and with guidance from the Gospels, we are to love God with all our heart, and Jesus is to be our counselor and friend in this relationship. As Jesus teaches, serving God is a spiritual practice in which he is the vine and we as Christians are the branches. Any relationship with nature is part of that relationship. From a Christian perspective this gives us clarity in our individual ecologies, as we are not then worshiping a certain bird, animal, or any other singular aspect of nature. However, in realizing the blessed way God created the world, and with Jesus' loving guidance, we may understand the oneness of all of life as this wonderful gift from God. We need nature to sustain life, and right now nature needs us to understand the way we relate to her has an overall effect on the balance of the relationship.

I often tell folks in worship that if a relationship or message becomes confusing, it is an indication one is getting off track. The idea of a living, loving God that Jesus teaches, and the requirement that we in turn should be gracious and loving towards ourselves and others, is quite simple. The care for, and relationship with, God's natural creation should be simple as well if we make sure we and our neighbors are loved in the process.

THE PEACE OF GOD

> Again Jesus said, "Peace be with you! As the Father has sent me, I am sending you." And with that he breathed on them and said, "Receive the Holy Spirit." (John 20:21–22)

As I have emphasized, relating with nature is relating with God and Jesus. This amazing life which is a gift from God is sustained by good things from God and the natural world. The reality is we need the natural world to sustain our lives in our current now. In past times and in the beginning, nature had the ability to reveal God. God's presence was in the clouds that filled the tabernacle tents of worship. Moses stood on holy ground. Jesus was baptized in the Jordan River, with a spirit of God descending on him like a dove, which changed his life, and he was transfigured on a mountain when he visited with Moses and Elijah.

Humanity has moved further and further from relating with the natural world. This separation from relating with the natural world is also a separation from a creator God and Jesus, through whom all things were made. It is that simple.

Yes, there are theories and theologies and thoughts that have facilitated this separation narrative. However, they are just that: thoughts. As noted of other fields of study which allow the sciences and historical research to correct their understanding for the betterment of humanity and hopefully also the natural world, should not the same be true for our own Christian worship? If humanity receives benefits from interacting with nature, is that a not showing of compassion and a following of Jesus who describes the neighbor in the story of the good Samaritan as the one who shows compassion? If the natural world benefits from humanity learning how to treat her with care and concern, is that not an action of mercy?

When we return to our human world after time relating with God and Jesus in nature, we bring a tangible spiritual feeling of peace. The science of the calming effects of nature on our cognitive and physical wellbeing affirms that peace. This peace Jesus offers his followers is help from God. Instead of reacting to everything in the world, such peace offers us a chance to open our hearts and seek this compassionate teaching from Jesus about loving God with all our hearts and neighbor as our selves.

The English definition of peace suggests stillness, tranquility, nonaction almost. Yet, given the way of God as creator and Jesus as the one through whom all things that have been made, is not peace alive in nature?

In the movement of the winds

In the green of the trees

In the life-giving waters

In the clouds

In the soil of the earth

In the food we eat and the songs of the birds

And hopefully within our relationships with our neighbors.

This practice of Christian spiritual ecology offers wellbeing to humanity and nature. It offers the chance to learn more about peace in our world. This is interconnectedness, the experience of oneness in self-realization, deep ecology, biophilia, the vast self, the forgotten song, inclusion, and Jesus as the Author of Life through whom all things have been made.

I imagine these aspects of the spiritual practice to be like the petals of a flower connecting to the heart center of the ecology relationship. Time in nature bestows humility, and humility bestows the fruits. The fruits give rise to thankfulness and giving, which then give rise to peace. This is much like the teaching from the natural world about how each ecological system supports the other in relationships. Such relationships reflect Jesus' teachings, for they are all about giving mercy, love, and goodness. These are the fruits of the heart.

Peace be with you.

Bibliography

American Lung Association. "Lung Association Launches Healthy and Efficient Homes Project to Promote Healthy Indoor Air Quality." August 15, 2023. https://www.lung.org/media/press-releases/on-average,-americans-spend-90-of-their-time-indo.

American Psychiatric Association. "American Adults Express Increased Anxiousness in Annual Poll." Psychiatry.org, May 1, 2024. https://www.psychiatry.org/news-room/news-releases/annual-poll-adults-express-increasing-anxiousness.

Anderson, Karen, and Colin Perrin. "Removed from Nature: The Modern Idea of Human Exceptionality." *Environmental Humanities* 10 (2018) 447–72. https://read.dukeupress.edu/environmental-humanities/article/10/2/447/136688/Removed-from-Nature-The-Modern-Idea-of-Human.

Bernstein, Ellen. *Ecology and the Jewish Spirit: Where Nature and the Sacred Meet.* Woodstock, VT: Jewish Lights, 2000.

Brown, Loretta Coleman. *What Makes You Come Alive.* Minneapolis: Broadleaf, 2023.

Buzzell, Linda, and Craig Chalquist, eds. *Ecotherapy: Healing with Nature in Mind.* San Francisco: Sierra Club, 2009.

Byrnes, Laurel. "Alexander Von Humboldt and the Interconnectedness of Nature." Biodiversity Heritage Library. https://blog.biodiversitylibrary.org/2020/10/alexander-von-humboldt.html.

Cobb, John B. Jr. *Is It Too Late? A Theology Of Ecology.* Minneapolis: Fortress, 2021.

Crawford, Amy. "Good Science Changes." University of Michigan School of Public Health, May 14, 2021. https://sph.umich.edu/findings/spring-2021/good-science-changes-thats-a-good-thing.html.

Dali Lama [Tenzin Gyatso], and Desmond Tutu. *The Book of Joy: Lasting Happiness in a Changing World.* New York: Penguin Random House, 2016.

Daughrity, Dryon B. *To Whom Does Christianity Belong?* Minneapolis: Fortress, 2015.

Delagran, Louise. "How Does Nature Impact Our Wellbeing?" Taking Charge of Your Wellbeing. https://www.takingcharge.csh.umn.edu/how-does-nature-impact-our-wellbeing.

DeVille, Nicole V., et al. "Time in Nature Is Associated with Increased Pro-Environmental Attitudes and Behaviors." *Int J Environ Res Public Health* 18 (2021) 7498. https://doi.org/10.3390/ijerph18147498.

Dixie, Quinton, and Peter Eisenstadt. "When Howard Thurman Met Mahatma Gandhi." Beacon Broadside, October 2, 2014. https://beaconbroadside.com/2014/10/02/when-howard-thurman-met-mahatma-gandhi-nonviolence-and-the-civil-rights-movement/

Earl E. Bakken Center for Spirituality & Healing. "Webinar: Nature Heals—An Intro to Nature-Based Therapeutics." YouTube, July 29, 2020. Video. https://www.youtube.com/watch?v=3a46Bk7vdiI.

Ecological Society of America. "What Is Ecology?" https://esa.org/about/what-does-ecology-have-to-do-with-me/.

Flinders, Tim. *John Muir: Spiritual Writings.* Maryknoll, NY: Orbis, 2013.

Jewish Virtual Library. "Issues in Jewish Ethics: Judaism's Rejection of Original Sin." https://jewishvirtuallibrary.org/history-wing/reference-relations/theological-debates-and-doctrinal-differences/judaism-s-rejection-of-original-sin.

Jordan, Rob. "Stanford Researches Find Mental Health Prescription: Nature." Stanford Report, June 30, 2015. https://news.stanford.edu/stories/2015/06/hiking-mental-health-063015.

Jorgensen, Kiara A., and Alan P. Padgett. *Ecotheology: A Christian Conversation.* Grand Rapids: Eerdmans, 2020.

Just, Felix. "On the Authorship of the Gospels and the Book of Revelation." Catholic Resources. https://catholic-resources.org/Bible/Eusebius_Gospels.htm.

Kumaria, Poonam. "Nature and Man: The Gandhian Concept of Deep Ecology." Mahatma Gandhi. https://www.mkgandhi.org/articles/natureman.php.

Li, Qing. *Forest Bathing: How Trees Can Help You Find Health and Happiness.* New York: Viking Random House, 2018.

Merriam-Webster. "Cosmology." https://www.merriam-webster.com/dictionary/cosmology.

Marina, Marko. "Who Wrote the Book of Revelation? The Surprising Answer!" Bart Ehrman, August 25, 2023. https://www.bartehrman.com/who-wrote-the-book-of-revelation/.

Marino, Lori. "The Scala Naturae Is Alive and Well in Modern Times." *HuffPost*, April 6, 2014. https://www.huffpost.com/entry/the-scala-naturae-is-aliv_b_471917.

McEwan, Kirsten, et al. "A Pragmatic Controlled Trial of Forest Bathing Compared with Compassionate Mind Training in the UK: Impacts on Self-Reported Wellbeing and Heart Rate Variability." *Sustainability* 13 (2021) 1380. https://doi.org/10.3390/su13031380.

McFague, Sallie. *Models of God: Theology for an Ecological, Nuclear Age.* Philadelphia: Fortress, 1988.

Minnesota Department of Health. "TV, Screen Time, and Health: Health Effects of Too Much Screen Time." April 18, 2024. https://www.health.state.mn.us/people/tvviewing/index.html.

Moses, Kara. "Spiritual Ecology: 10 Practices to Reawaken the Sacred in Everyday Life." *The Ecologist*, July 17, 2017. https://theecologist.org/2017/jul/17/spiritual-ecology-10-practices-reawaken-sacred-everyday-life.

NASA Science. "The Causes of Climate Change." https://science.nasa.gov/climate-change/causes/.

National Geographic. "Before the Flood." https://www.natgeotv.com/uk/shows/natgeo/before-the-flood.

Newell, Phillip J. *Christ of the Celts: The Healing of Creation.* Glasgow, UK: Wild Goose, 2008.

Nielsen, John. "Americans Spending Less Time in Nature." NPR, February 6, 2008. https://www.npr.org/2008/02/06/18698731/americans-spending-less-time-in-nature.

Open Horizons. "A Need for the Mystical." https://www.openhorizons.org/a-need-for-the-mystical-why-process-theology-needs-howard-thurman.html.

Padowitz, Joel, and Jonathan Sassen. "Sacred Science: Judaism's Perspective on Studying the Natural World." Aish, September 15, 2024. https://aish.com/sacred-science-judaisms-perspective-on-studying-the-natural-world/.

Richardson, Miles, and Kirsten McEwan. "30 Days Wild and the Engagement with Nature Beauty, Nature Connectedness and Wellbeing." *Frontiers in Psychology* 9 (2018) 1500. https://doi.org/10.3389/fpsyg.2018.01500.

Ridberg, Rabbi Yael. "Sin and Forgiveness." Reconstructing Judaism. https://www.reconstructingjudaism.org/article/sin-and-forgiveness/.

Sanneh, Lamin. *Whose Religion Is Christianity?* Grand Rapids: Eerdmans, 2003.

Shvat, Ari. "Original Sin in Judaism." Yeshiva.co. https://www.yeshiva.co/ask/54744.

Simpson, Ray. *Celtic Christianity: Deep Roots for a Modern Faith.* Vestal, NY: Anamchara, 2014.

Stoll, Mark R. "God and John Muir: A Psychological Interpretation of John Muir's Life and Religion." Sierra Club. https://vault.sierraclub.org/john_muir_exhibit/life/god_john_muir_mark_stoll.aspx.

Summers, James K., and Deborah N. Vivian. "Ecotherapy—A Forgotten Ecosystem Service: A Review." *Frontiers in Psychology* 9 (2018) 1389. https://doi.org/10.3389/fpsyg.2018.01389.

Sweeney, Jon M. *Francis of Assisi, In His Own Words.* Brewster, MA: Paraclete, 2013.

United Nations. "What Is Climate Change?" https://www.un.org/en/climatechange/what-is-climate-change.

University of Derby. "Nature Connectedness Research Group." https://www.derby.ac.uk/research/themes/zero-carbon/zero-carbon-nbs-research-centre/nature-connectedness-research-group/.

US Fish and Wildlife Service. "New Study Shows Americans' Deep Appreciation for Nature, Barriers to Connection." https://www.fws.gov/press-release/2017-04/new-study-shows-americans-deep-appreciation-nature-barriers-connection.

Vainio, Olli-Pekka. *Cosmology in Theological Perspective: Understanding Our Place in the Universe.* Grand Rapids: Baker, 2018.

Von Humboldt, Alexander. *Views of Nature.* Chicago: The University of Chicago Press, 2014.

Weir, Kirsten. "Nurtured by Nature." *Monitor on Psychology* 51 (2020) 50. https://www.apa.org/monitor/2020/04/nurtured-nature.

United Nations. "What Is Climate Change?" https://www.un.org/en/climatechange/what-is-climate-change.

Whitehead, Alfred North. *Process and Reality.* New York: Free Press, 1929.

Wilson, Edward O. *Biophilia.* London: Harvard University Press, 1984.

Yale Forum on Religion and Ecology. "Christianity Introduction." https://fore.yale.edu/Publications/Books/Religions-World-and-Ecology-Book-Series/Christianity-Table-Contents/Christianity.

www.ingramcontent.com/pod-product-compliance
Lightning Source LLC
LaVergne TN
LVHW020639100826
845148LV00012B/2251